THE 1972 HOCKEY SHOWDOWN

Tell me the story, Gramps!

Andrew Kavchak

Other books by the author:

Chess Kid: The Quest for the Cup

Westminster School: Reflections of a Boarder

Waiting for a National Autism Strategy

*The Fight for Autism Treatment in Canada:
Reflections of a Parent Activist*

*Remembering Gouzenko:
The Struggle to Honour a Cold War Hero*

Katyn Grandson: No Permission to Forget

*The Katyn Forest Massacre:
An Annotated Bibliography of Books in English*

A Guide to 75 Selected Holocaust History Books

Dying Echoes: Memoirs of the War 1914-1920
By Stanisław Kawczak
Introduction by Andrew Kavchak

This book is dedicated to
the players and coaches of Team Canada 1972.
You guys were the best.
Ever.
Period.

CONTENTS

INTRODUCTION

Something special happened in September 1972. It was big.

Really big.

The hockey "Summit Series" between Canada and the Soviet Union was a first ever clash between the best Canadian hockey players who played in the NHL and the best Soviet players who played on their national team. The whole point of the series was to determine who was the real best. The series involved eight games. The first four were played at the beginning of the month in Canada. The last four were played at the end of the month in Moscow. Despite having only one win and a tie in the first five games and having the odds stacked against them in Moscow, Team Canada staged the most dramatic comeback in Canadian sports history.

Canadians who were alive at the time will never forget the emotional roller coaster ride that started with the disastrous first game and lasted right up to the very end of the final one. The unbearable tension and suspense that built up throughout the month was only resolved when the outcome of the series was finally determined in the last minute of the last period of the last game. Once over, the series left me, and a lot of other Canadians, emotionally drained and exhausted. The Team Canada saga in that Summit Series said a lot about team spirit. It is hard to find a better story of grit and determination in any sport. I was nine years old in

September 1972. By the time the series was over I considered the members of Team Canada 1972 to be Hockey Gods. Over half a century later, I still do.

Exciting? Nothing has come close since.

Inspiring? You can say that again.

Made you proud to be a Canadian? You better believe it!

Out of Canada's population of 22 million at the time some 16 million watched the final game on September 28, 1972. When was the last time the whole country effectively shut down in the middle of a weekday to watch a hockey game? When, since World War II, was Canada ever so united about anything?

Over the years I have often asked many younger Canadians whether they were familiar with the history of the Canada–USSR hockey Summit Series of 1972. Many recognized the photograph of Paul Henderson jumping in celebration after scoring the final goal of the series. However, few knew the background or the milestone events that took place throughout the series leading up to that famous goal and the jubilation captured in the famous photograph. As time goes by more and more Canadians know less and less about it.

This book is meant for young Canadians of today and tomorrow. I hope it will contribute to the preservation of our collective memory of that monumental Summit Series and spark some interest in its history among future generations of Canadian youth.

Andrew Kavchak
Ottawa, Canada.
July 1, 2023.

CHAPTER 1:
FIFTY YEARS LATER

Andy was looking forward to spending the Labour Day long weekend with his grandparents, Floyd and Denise, at their cottage in the Laurentians. It was Friday, 2 September 2022, and Monday would be a holiday. The summer holidays were ending and it would be back to school for Andy and his classmates on Tuesday. That Friday afternoon Andy's parents dropped him off at his grandparents' home in the Outremont neighbourhood of Montreal. Floyd and Denise already had their car packed with supplies and were ready to leave town and head up North with Andy as soon as they could to beat the rush hour traffic. Normally Andy's parents would go to the cottage too but this weekend they planned to stay behind and paint some rooms at home, including Andy's bedroom, so that it would all be done by Monday.

Spending the weekend and summer holidays in the Laurentians was a long-standing tradition for Montreal cottage-goers. Decades earlier many would take the train. Then cars and paved highways provided the primary means of transportation. The main train line fell into disuse and was paved over into a bike path that stretches over 150 kilometres. The biggest change these days is the appearance of more and more electric vehicles on the highway.

Floyd drove a trusty old Toyota Camry and made sure to fill the gas tank before they left town. Andy and his grandparents arrived at the cottage after about an hour and a half on the road. They unloaded the car and Andy brought his bag to the small guest room that was his whenever he visited.

Andy was eleven years old and had blond hair and blue eyes. He was of average height for a kid his age. He did his homework diligently and got good grades, but like most boys, he was more interested in playing with friends, engaging in sports, and having fun. When Andy was not amongst friends, he frequently spent time on his iPhone and kept in touch by texting them.

Denise prepared dinner for the three of them. "So Andy, are you looking forward to school next week?" Floyd asked at the dinner table.

"Yeah, it'll be great to see my friends again. I'll be in Grade 6 this year. I also can't wait for the hockey tryouts next weekend. I've been practicing my shots in the driveway all summer and I'm getting better. I hope to make the 'A' team this year."

Andy had been playing hockey for a few years. His parents started taking him to public skating at the local arena in their Notre-Dame-de-Grâce neighbourhood when he was four years old. When he was five, they registered him in the local minor hockey association's program for beginners. Every year at the beginning of September the association evaluates the skill level of all the kids at different age levels and assigns them to appropriate teams. Andy loved being on a team with many of his friends from the neighbourhood and playing games throughout the hockey season with other teams that were in the league.

"Oh, of course! I forgot about that. It's the start of the hockey season," Floyd said. "Good luck with the tryouts, Andy. I hope you get on a team that you like and have a good coach. You know, I've been thinking a lot about hockey today, but it wasn't about the upcoming season."

"What were you thinking about?" Andy asked.

"This morning while I had my morning coffee, I checked some news websites and one of the headlines caught my eye. It reminded me that today is a special anniversary of a special event in hockey history."

"What was it? Did the Canadiens win a Stanley Cup or something?"

"No, it wasn't the Stanley Cup. Something else that was really special happened in September a half century ago."

"A half century ago? Fifty years? That would have been 1972. What happened then?" Andy wondered.

"Actually, September 2, 1972, was the start of something that lasted the whole month and had the attention of every hockey fan in Canada at the time."

Denise knew what Floyd was referring to but said nothing, not wanting to spoil the story that she knew he wanted to tell.

"I was twelve years old at the time and in Grade 7," Floyd said. He sighed and smiled before adding, "I'm 62 now and I still remember it like it was yesterday."

"So what was it, Gramps? Now I'm curious. Tell me." Andy was starting to get impatient.

"You know what it was," Floyd said playfully. "You'll have to guess."

Andy had no idea what the event was but enjoyed the banter with his grandfather. "Aw, c'mon Gramps! Can you at least give me a hint?" Andy asked.

"Okay. Here's the hint. I have a framed photograph hanging on the wall in my study at home. That's a giveaway. Now you should know it!"

Andy thought about it for a second and said "It's the one of Paul Henderson after he scored a big goal," Andy said with relief. "I got it! That was in the Canada-Russia hockey series in 1972, right?"

"That's the one!" Floyd said while Andy beamed with satisfaction. "Today is the fiftieth anniversary of the first game of the series. That first game took place at the Montreal Forum on Saturday, 2 September 1972. I was a little older than you at the time and was just about to start a new school year at Collège Stanislas in Outremont. But unlike you, I did not play hockey. I just loved watching the Montreal Canadiens team with your great-grandfather every Saturday night on television. Before the series started a lot of people thought Team Canada would blow the Russians away. One team sure got blown away, but it wasn't the Russians. They taught the Canadians a lesson in humility. After that first game, the whole country was in shock. I remember the next day. It was a Sunday and I thought it was the worst day of my life."

"But Canada ended up winning the series, right? That's what you told me before," Andy asked.

"Oh, sure. Yes, we did. But that whole month of September 1972 was a roller coaster of a ride. We would not know the outcome until the last minute of the final game of the series at the end of the month. When it was finally over, I thought the players on Team Canada were the greatest, and I was so proud of Team Canada and proud to be a Canadian."

"So the picture of Henderson jumping up is your souvenir of that series, eh Gramps?" Andy called his grandfather 'Gramps'. He called his grandmother Denise 'Grandma'."

"It sure is, but that photograph is more than just a souvenir."

"What do you mean?"

"Life is full of challenges. You will be confronted with challenges, one after another, all your life. How individuals and groups of people respond to challenges reflects who they are. During the series with the Russians, there was a period when the circumstances were looking pretty grim and many Canadians gave up on the Canadian team. But the players on the team didn't throw in the towel! They took a 'never surrender' approach and persevered with determination. The players on that team had faith in themselves and fought to the very end. That's the way winners play. They demonstrated courage, resilience, and fortitude in difficult circumstances. That team demonstrated team spirit better than any sports team that I can remember. That photograph more than any other one that I've ever seen captures and reflects the will to win. That photograph of Henderson celebrating is one of the most well-known photographs in the history of Canadian sports. When I look at it, it is not just a photograph of Henderson celebrating after scoring a big goal. I see a lot more than that. I see the whole series, from the terrible start through to the comeback that I thought at the time was something close to a miracle. To me, that photograph represents Team Canada's character and its spirit of determination and guts. I love that photograph and have always had a framed copy on a wall at home. It never fails to inspire me."

"You know Gramps, I've heard you talk about the 1972 series and Henderson's goal, but you never told me the whole story of what happened throughout that month. I know they lost the first game, but what happened in the second game and all the other games? How many games were there?"

"Oh! Oh! Now you're going to get your grandfather started!" Denise interjected as she got up from the table and went to the kitchen. "Don't get him going on the series unless you're prepared to listen to the whole story. If there's one thing that your grandfather is guaranteed to get excited about, it's that 1972 hockey series. Sometimes your grandfather gets so animated when he tells people about it that he becomes a kid again."

"Why haven't you or my dad told me the whole story before?" Andy asked.

"I told your father the story so many times when he was a kid that when he was older, he told me on several occasions that he already knew it and kind of got fed up with my talking about it so often. Later, he told me that since I knew more about it than he did, he thought it would be better that I tell you the story when you were old enough and were interested because you'd probably enjoy it more hearing it from me than him. I haven't told you the whole story yet because you were young and would probably not understand the details or be interested in the off-ice shenanigans that were such a big part of the whole drama. I think the history of the Summit Series is one that every young Canadian hockey player should know. It's an unusual story. It's also very entertaining and it has some life lessons in it for everyone. I guess you're old enough now to appreciate it. What do you say, Andy? Are you interested? Are you ready?"

"Yeah! Tell me the story, Gramps!"

"Great! I'm glad you want to hear it. And this anniversary is a perfect occasion to talk about it."

"When do we start?" Andy asked.

"Tomorrow morning after breakfast we'll go for a canoe ride around the lake and I'll start telling you about it then. I'll need to give you some background and history first so that you will understand the context in which the series was played. After that, we'll go through the whole series game by game. This will take me back in time but I never tire of telling the story to anyone interested."

"You're going to get a history lesson unlike anything you'd get in school, Andy!" Denise said.

"Good. I like hockey stories from the good ol' days!"

CHAPTER 2:
SETTING THE STAGE

"So Andy, are you looking forward to getting out on the lake with the Grumman?" Floyd asked the next morning over breakfast. Floyd had an old aluminum canoe made by a company called Grumman. He loved that canoe and even though it had accumulated some dents over the years, it was as solid as when it was new. The weather was warm and there was hardly any wind. The conditions were perfect for canoeing.

"Sure am, Gramps! And I'm looking forward to your telling me what happened back in '72!" Andy replied enthusiastically.

"Good! I'll tell you the story while we make our way around the lake," Floyd said. While cleaning the table with Andy's help, he added, "Let's fill our water bottles and bring some snacks to munch on." Before going outside Floyd asked, "What else do we need besides lifejackets and paddles?"

"Sunscreen and a hat" Andy remembered.

"Exactly," Floyd replied. As they got ready to head out the door Floyd said "Denise, we'll be back in a while."

"Have fun gentlemen. And make sure you both keep your life jackets on," Denise reminded them. She always worried about things like that.

"Don't worry, Grandma. We always wear them," Andy replied.

Andy sat at the front of the canoe while Floyd set himself up at the back. The lake had a large circular shape with cottages along the shore all around. Floyd proposed that they paddle out from the shore a distance and then in a clockwise fashion around the lake. Once they were in the canoe and paddling in a steady rhythm Andy asked "So tell me about the 1972 series, Gramps. What happened?"

"Okay. Let's set the stage with some hockey history so that you can understand the context within which the series occurred. The world has changed a lot since 1972, but you have to go back even further to understand what the series was all about. From the beginning when Canadians started to play hockey, we believed that we were the best hockey players in the world. The very first indoor game in the world was played in Montreal in 1875, so we had a lot of experience. And the best Canadian hockey players played in the National Hockey League [NHL]. From the 1940s until 1967 the NHL had only six teams. Do you know which teams they were?"

"The Montreal Canadiens, Toronto Maple Leafs, Boston Bruins, Detroit Red Wings, Chicago Blackhawks, and one more but I'm not sure which one," Andy replied.

"Hey! That's pretty good! The sixth team was the New York Rangers. And guess where the majority of the players in the league were from?"

"They were Canadians!" Andy spontaneously blurted out.

"That's right! The vast majority were Canadians. And then in 1967, the league expanded to 12 teams to include Los Angeles, Oakland, Minnesota, St. Louis, Philadelphia, and Pittsburgh. Again, the vast majority of the players were Canadians. By the 1990s the league had expanded to the point where there were so many teams and so many players that I have no idea who's who and what's what anymore. But when I was your age, we knew almost all the players and could easily recognize them on television. Very few of the players wore helmets and you could recognize some of the players just by their hair! At that time the goalies had just started using masks to protect their faces! I remember when I was a kid the Minnesota North Stars goalie, Gump Worsley, still didn't wear a mask so you could see his face."

"Wow. I don't think any goalie would do that today."

"I don't think so either. Canadians knew that we were the best hockey players in North America, but the only way to show that we were the best in the world was to prove it on the international stage. And that's what Canada did starting over a century ago. International hockey competitions took place at the World Championships and the Olympics. The International Ice Hockey Federation [IIHF] organizes the World Championships every year and the Olympics games are held every four years. However, sometimes they were combined so that if a country won the gold medal at the Olympics it also won the World Championship. Canada dominated and won the gold medal at the World Championships most of the time throughout the 1920s and 1930s and for a period after World War II. Similarly, before World War II the Canadians tended to win the gold medals at the Olympics. After the war, we won gold in 1948 and 1952. The next time we would win an Olympic gold medal in hockey after that was in 2002!"

"Fifty years later?!"

"That's right, fifty years."

"Why? What happened?" Andy asked.

"Something happened that changed the nature of international competition. We suddenly had a new competitor who was very good and made proving Canada to be the best on the world stage a lot more difficult."

"It was the Russians, right?"

"Exactly," Floyd replied. "Have you heard the term 'Soviet Union' before?"

"Kinda. But I'm not really sure what it was," Andy replied.

"Well, Russia is a huge country with a long history. The country was led by a tsar and in 1917 the tsar was overthrown in a revolution. The communists came to power and they tried to create a different political and economic system. Over the years Russia incorporated several neighbouring countries into their country and called them Soviet Socialist Republics. Altogether, they called the whole country the 'Union of Soviet Socialist Republics' and the acronym was 'USSR'. The short form was 'Soviet Union'. Russia was the biggest and most powerful nation and republic within the Soviet Union. Many people in the West just called people from the Soviet Union 'Russians' but that was not necessarily accurate since they may not have been Russians but from some other nationality or republic in the Soviet Union. The communists preferred to refer to all the citizens of the Soviet Union as 'Soviets'. The Soviet Union disintegrated in the early 1990s and all the republics became independent countries, including Russia. Even though many books refer to the players on the Soviet national team as 'Russians', I'll be referring to them as the 'Soviets'."

"Gotcha," Andy said as he continued paddling.

"Anyway, right after WWII the Soviets decided to start a national hockey program and develop their best players for international competition. And guess what happened?"

"What?"

"In 1954 the Soviets participated for the first time in the World Championships and won the gold medal."

"Whoa! They got to the top of the hockey world that fast?"

"Yup. And they won it again in 1956. And then they won it every year from 1963 to 1971."

"What happened to Canada then? Why weren't we winning?" Andy asked.

"I'll tell you why. It was because the people who ran the Olympics and the World Championships had a rule that only amateurs could compete. Professional players were not allowed to participate in those tournaments."

"What's the difference between an amateur and a professional?" Andy asked.

"Amateurs are athletes who engage in sports for the joy of competing and don't get paid. They have other principal activities like going to school or working for a living and can only devote a portion of their time to training and competing. On the other hand, professional athletes get paid for playing their sport. That's their full-time job. They spend their time either training or playing the sport and competing. As a result of their focusing on their training and playing with others who do the same, they tend to play at a higher standard than amateurs."

"Okay, I see," Andy said.

"Canada's best hockey players were professionals who played in the NHL and none of them were allowed to compete in the World Championships or the Olympics."

"So who did we send to represent Canada at those tournaments?" Andy wondered.

"Every year the Canadian Amateur Hockey Association, known as the CAHA, would choose an amateur team to represent Canada. However, instead of putting a team together of the best Canadian amateur players from across the country, they usually picked a team that had just won a championship. That's how things more or less worked from 1920 until 1963. For example, the Edmonton Mercurys won the World Championship in 1950 and 1952, the Lethbridge Maple Leafs won it in 1951, the Penticton Vees won it in 1955, and the Whitby Dunlops won it in 1958."

"I never heard of those teams before," Andy said.

"They were amazing teams of Canadian amateurs. However, none of those teams were composed of the best Canadian amateur players from across the country. Do you see the problem?

"What problem?"

"Teams that won Canadian championships were good, but the best amateur players could have been on different teams across the country. Imagine if Canada could have picked the best amateur all-stars from across the country and molded them into a national team. Some people thought Canada needed a national team program to at least try to do that."

"I see. So did we get a national team program going?" Andy asked.

"Yes. Around 1963 a Canadian priest named Father David Bauer founded a national team program to try to improve the situation."

"Who was he?"

"David Bauer was a Canadian hockey player who was offered a playing contract with the Boston Bruins when he was only 15 but he followed his father's advice and declined the offer to pursue his education. He eventually became a priest while continuing to play and coach hockey. He set up a national team program and his team competed at the 1964 Winter Olympics."

"How did they do?"

"Canada was shut out of the ice hockey medals for the first time in Olympic history. The national team program continued until 1969 but the Canadian team did not win any Olympic or World Championship gold medals which was a disappointment. While Canada's dwindling fortunes at the Olympics and World Championships was largely due to our best professionals not being allowed to compete in international games, the Soviets had no such problem."

"How did they do that?" Andy asked in a surprised tone.

"The Soviets simply insisted that they did not have any professionals and that all their best hockey players who played in international tournaments were amateurs."

"Were they amateurs?"

"No, they weren't but the international hockey authorities repeatedly let them get away with it. In 1972 the premier Soviet hockey league had nine teams that were composed of the best Soviet players. As with everything in the Soviet society, each team was effectively supported by the state although each team was technically affiliated and supported by various army clubs, institutions, trade unions or factories."

"What about their national team?"

"The Soviet national team was composed of the best players from the league. However, the vast majority were from the Moscow Central Army Club. About 15 players on the Soviet national team in the 1972 series came from that Central Army team. The core of the Soviet national team was always playing together. Those Soviet hockey players spent all their time training to be the best hockey players they could be and they did it for eleven months of the year."

"Eleven months of the year!?" Andy was stunned. "I wish I could play hockey that much! What about the NHL players? How much did they play?"

"NHL players attended training camps in September and the season would start in October. The 1971–72 NHL regular season ended on April 2, 1972. The top teams would keep playing in the playoffs for another month or so. The Stanley Cup was awarded to the Boston Bruins on May 11, 1972. The NHL players stopped playing hockey as soon as their teams were finished for the year. NHL players took the summer off and played golf unless they ran a hockey school or worked on a family farm or something. Most players would start the September training camp in poor shape and their conditioning would improve as the regular season progressed until it peaked at the end of the season and the playoffs when it counted most."

"So were the Soviet hockey players more professional than the Canadians?" Andy asked.

"In terms of the amount of time they spent training and playing, absolutely," Floyd said. "The Soviet insistence that all their players were amateurs was meant to ensure their best players played in international competitions and maximize their chances of winning. When the 1972 series was being set up the players from both teams had to obtain visas that would permit them to go and play in the games in the other country. When the Soviets submitted their team's official visa applications to the Canadian embassy in Moscow, what do you think they listed as the principal occupations of their National Team members?

"What?"

"Almost all of them claimed to be students! Their country's best players claimed to be college kids. The Canadian coach wrote that before the series he met with the Soviet coaches and scouts and they told him that the Soviet players practiced on the ice for two hours every morning, ate lunch, slept, and then returned refreshed to the ice for evening practice. If they were students, when would they attend any classes or do their homework with such a schedule?"

"Yeah, when?" Andy said bewildered.

"Lawrence Martin was a Canadian journalist who reported from Moscow for a while and in his 1990 book, *The Red Machine: The Soviet Quest to Dominate Canada's Game* he included a chapter about the Soviet view of the 1972 series. In it he quoted Yevgeni Zimin, one of the Soviet national team members who scored the first Soviet goal of the series, as saying that the players on the Soviet national team played and practiced for eleven months of the year and didn't have a chance to do anything else because they had no time. Zimin said they had to be paid by somebody and it was by their government and by numerous sports organizations. He said they were professionals in every sense of the word. So once the Soviets started participating in international hockey tournaments their phony amateurs frequently beat our real amateurs. By the end of the 1960s, the Canadian hockey authorities had enough of the unfair situation."

"What did they do about it, Gramps?" Andy wondered.

"In 1969 Canada withdrew from any participation in the World Championships and Olympics," Floyd explained.

"Whoa! Canada did not play hockey in the international competitions?"

"Nope. At the time the federal government also created an organization called Hockey Canada to try, among other things, to get the IIHF to allow Canada's professionals to participate in international hockey."

"Did it work?" Andy wondered.

"Not for a long time. In the meantime, Canada did not participate in the hockey competitions at the 1972 or 1976 Olympics and the boycott of IIHF World Championships lasted until 1977."

"But what about the 1972 series with the Soviets? How did that happen?" Andy asked.

"Since the Soviets had arrived on the scene there had always been a desire to see our best players play against theirs. Eventually, an agreement was negotiated by representatives from Hockey Canada and the CAHA with the Soviet hockey authorities in April 1972. What they agreed to was a series of games that would include the best players from both countries. The games were supposed to be exhibition games. However, everyone knew that this series would finally settle the question of who were the best hockey players on the planet and the games were not going to be just friendly scrimmages. Everything was on the line and both sides were going to play to win. The terms of the initial agreement consisted of a series of eight games to be played in September later that year. The first four games would be in Canada and the last four in the Soviet Union. It was also eventually arranged for the Canadian team to play two exhibition games in Stockholm with the Swedish national team between the games in Canada and Moscow. After the final game with the Soviets in Moscow the Canadians would then play a game in Prague with the Czechoslovak national team before returning home to Canada.

The agreement was that the games would be under the IIHF international rules instead of NHL rules. That included the international system of officiating with only two officials on the ice instead of three like in the NHL. American referees would officiate the games in Canada and European referees would officiate the games in Moscow.

When it was announced that there was going to be a hockey series with the Soviets, the whole country got excited. The series became known as the 'Summit Series' and the country would be represented by 'Team Canada'. The media and newspapers started to talk about it throughout the summer. However, the Canadian organizers had some things to do. Once the agreement was finalized, what do you think were the first steps in getting a team together?"

"Picking the players?" Andy guessed.

"Who's going to do that?"

"The coach?"

"Right. So the first thing hockey authorities had to do was pick a coach. And they picked a great one."

"Who?"

"Harry Sinden."

"Who was he?"

"Harry Sinden had played junior hockey in Oshawa. He had a job with General Motors and played senior amateur hockey for the Whitby-Dunlops. Over five years his team won a provincial championship and two national championships. In 1958 his team went to Oslo for the World Championships and beat the Soviets 4-2 in the gold medal game. In 1960 Sinden was on the Canadian team that beat the Soviets at the Olympics 9-3 but then lost to the Americans and finished with a silver medal. Sinden became the coach of the Boston Bruins in the late sixties and they won the Stanley Cup in 1970. After that victory, he expected a pay increase and quit coaching when he wasn't satisfied with his remuneration. When the series was announced Sinden was an obvious choice. He had experience playing at the international level and had played against the Soviets. He proved he could coach a Stanley Cup-winning team. He was also available while the other NHL coaches would be busy at their teams' training camps in September preparing for the coming NHL season. One of the things Sinden insisted on was that if he was picked to be the coach, he would have to have control over the team and be free from any interference so he could do things his way. He got the job. The first thing Sinden did was pick his assistant coach."

"Who did he pick?

"He chose John Ferguson."

"I never heard of him either," Andy said.

"Ferguson had played for the Montreal Canadiens during the 1960s and retired in 1971. I remember watching Ferguson on television when I was a kid. He was one of those enforcer-type of guys who would not hesitate to get into a fight if someone pushed one of his teammates around. Ferguson was the type of guy that whether you liked him or not you would prefer to have him on your team than play against him. The funny thing about Ferguson was that even though I disliked fighters in the NHL, he gave the impression that he was actually a nice guy off the ice. Sinden knew Ferguson would be a great assistant coach even though he had never coached before. Ferguson was allergic to losing and always motivated everyone on his team. None of the players would be allowed to even think about losing.

Once Ferguson accepted Sinden's offer to be the assistant coach, the next job was to recruit players to make the team. First, the coaches had to decide how many players to invite. The agreed upon rules for the series were that each team could only dress 19 players for each game. Normally a coach would add a few more players to have some spares in case of injuries during the series. However, Sinden and Ferguson decided to invite twice as many to be on the team. In the end, there were about thirty-five players."

"Why so many?" Andy asked.

"Sinden wanted the players to be able to scrimmage during the training camp in August and have two teams playing each other for practice. They could not play against any other team of their calibre because none of the other NHL teams were available before September. However, Sinden did not invite the players to tryout for the team. If they accepted the invitation they were on the team. He planned to change the players in the lineup for each game so that everyone would be able to play at least once in the series."

"So who did they pick to be on the team?"

"Players that they considered the best in the NHL for each of the positions on the team. When the team was announced I recognized most of the names. By the end of the series, I knew all their names and so did all the other hockey fans across Canada."

"You still remember them, Gramps? After all these years?"

"Of course! Who forgets their childhood heroes? The biggest group from one NHL team was the six players from my favourite Montreal Canadiens. The Montreal players on the team were Yvan Cournoyer, the Mahovlich brothers, Serge Savard, Guy Lapointe, and Ken Dryden. My favourite hockey player was Yvan Cournoyer who played right wing and started with the Canadiens in 1963. His nickname was 'The Roadrunner' because he was so fast. By the time he retired in 1979, he had ten Stanley Cup championship rings."

"Wow! He won ten Stanley Cups?!"

"Yup! One ring for each finger. On the forward line, there were also Frank and Pete Mahovlich. Frank was six feet tall and his younger brother was six feet, five inches. When Pete was on skates, he was a giant. Both were left-wingers and exceptional players. However, they had different personalities. Frank seemed to be a serious guy while Pete was more of a joker who liked to have fun.

Serge Savard was a defenceman who joined the Canadiens in 1966. In his second full NHL season, he became the first defenceman to win the Conn Smythe Trophy as the playoffs' most valuable player. The other defenceman from the Canadiens was Guy Lapointe who started playing with the team during the 1968-1969 season. Lapointe had a reputation for powerful slapshots and bodychecks.

One of the goalies named to the team was Ken Dryden. Dryden's story is unbelievable. In 1971 he joined the Canadiens at the end of the season and played six games with the team. The Canadiens won all six and Dryden continued playing with the team in the playoffs. They ended up winning the Stanley Cup. He also won the Conn Smythe Trophy as the most valuable player during the playoffs. At the end of the next 1971-72 season Dryden won the Calder Trophy as rookie of the year. He managed to qualify as a rookie since he did not play enough games the previous year to qualify as a rookie at that time! He went on to play with the Canadiens until 1979 and won five more Stanley Cups. Dryden was tall and would often stand up straight and lean on his stick while the action was at the other end of the rink. There is a huge statue of him in that pose in the Hockey Hall of Fame."

"Who else was on the team, Gramps?"

"Five players on Team Canada were from the Boston Bruins. Phil Esposito played centre and was a scoring machine. He was a big guy who tended to hang around in front of the net where he was always a threat. His teammates were Wayne Cashman who was a left-winger, two defencemen, Don Awrey and Bobby Orr, and the Bruins' goalie Ed Johnston."

"I know Bobby Orr. You told me before that he was one of the greatest players ever," Andy said confidently.

"He sure was. Bobby Orr was a sensation who revolutionized the game by showing how a defenceman could contribute to the offense. When the Boston Bruins scouts first saw him play in a Pee Wee tournament, they began to court him and his parents. He ended up being drafted by Boston and helped them win the Stanley Cup in 1970 and 1972. Before Orr came on the scene, defencemen were not expected to go far beyond the opponent's blue line when the team was on the offensive. Bobby Orr changed all that. He could be behind his own net one minute and a few seconds later he would be doing a wrap-around and scoring at the other end of the ice. He also accomplished something that was considered inconceivable before and which has not been replicated since."

"What's that, Gramps?"

"In 1970 he won the NHL's scoring title. Can you believe that? He is the only defenceman in the league's history to score the most points in goals and assists in an NHL season! And guess what?"

"What?"

"He did it again in 1975! Not once, but twice he scored more points than anyone else in the league and he was a defenceman! Bobby Orr was simply the best defenceman in NHL history and one of the greatest hockey players ever. The games my father and I enjoyed watching the most at that time were those between Montreal and Boston. Watching Phil Esposito and Bobby Orr playing together was like watching a magic show on ice. I remember that the rivalry between Boston and Montreal was intense in those days and whenever they played against each other we knew there would be fireworks. Unfortunately, Bobby Orr had some problems with his knee. He joined Team Canada but it was not clear if he would be able to play in the series. However, just his being there was a source of inspiration for the other players.

There were also a few players from the Chicago Blackhawks including goalie Tony Esposito who was Phil's younger brother, Stan Mikita, Dennis Hull, Bill White, and Pat Stapleton. There were five players from the New York Rangers. The three forwards were Jean Ratelle, Vic Hadfield, and Rod Gilbert who were known as the GAG line."

"GAG line? What did that mean?"

"GAG stood for 'Goal-a-Game'. There were also two defencemen from the Rangers, Rod Seiling and Brad Park. Park began playing for the Rangers in 1968 and was considered one of the best defencemen of his era. If Bobby Orr had not been playing at that time Brad Park would have probably been considered the best."

"What about the Leafs? Did Toronto have any players on Team Canada?" Andy asked.

"They sure did. Brian Glennie, Ron Ellis, and Paul Henderson. I did not recognize the name of Brian Glennie, but I sure knew Ellis and Henderson. There was always a rivalry between Toronto and Montreal and the Leafs had some great players. Sinden's picking Ellis and Henderson for the team was a stroke of genius. The four players from the Detroit Red Wings were Gary Bergman, Red Berenson, Mickey Redmond, and Marcel Dionne."

"That sounds like a lot of players, Gramps. Were there any others?"

"There sure were. It was a big team! There was one player from the Philadephia Flyers named Bobby Clarke; two players from the Minnesota North Stars, Bill Goldsworthy and Jean-Paul Parisé; two players from the Buffalo Sabres, Gilbert Perreault and Richard Martin; and there were two from the Vancouver Canucks, Dale Tallon and Jocelyn Guevremont. All the players were invited to come to the training camp and join the team. However, in the end, some of them did not end up playing much, if at all, in any games during the series."

"When did they get together to practice and prepare for the series?" Andy asked.

"Before the training camp started Sinden had some important business to straighten out about the series. In July he flew to Moscow with four other team officials to meet their Soviet counterparts to see if they could resolve and clarify a few matters. The other four Canadians were Ferguson, Alan Eagleson, Bob Haggert, and Mike Cannon. Together they ran the Team Canada operations throughout the series and Sinden called the group 'Team Five'. Alan Eagleson was the head of the NHL Players' Association which was formed in 1967. Eagleson was also a key figure in the Hockey Canada organization who helped organize the series and acted as the team's troubleshooter and chief negotiator with Soviets authorities throughout the series. Mike Cannon was Eagleson's executive assistant. Bob Haggert served as Sinden's executive assistant. The Soviets that they met in Moscow included the Soviet national coach, Vsevolod Bobrov, and his assistant coach, Boris Kulagin."

"What did Sinden want to talk about?"

"He found that some of the terms of the initial April agreement gave the Soviets an advantage. He didn't like the timing of the series which guaranteed that the Canadians would be out-of-shape but he knew he could not do anything about that. However, he also didn't like the use of the international rules and the international officiating system with which the NHL players were unfamiliar. He also wanted to discuss the scouting provisions for both sides."

"Why did the Canadians agree to something that was a disadvantage?" Andy wondered.

"The negotiators of the April agreement probably assumed that the Canadian players could beat the Soviets at any time and under any rules. They were perhaps too overconfident. Regarding the officiating of the games, Sinden had played under the international system and was convinced that it was inferior to the NHL system. In the international system, only two officials are used and both are considered referees with equal authority. Sinden did not think a game could be handled properly with two bosses. He thought that there should only be one person who makes final decisions. In the NHL three officials are used. There are two linesmen for offside and icing calls. That frees the one referee to watch for penalties and he has the final say. Under the international system, both referees are responsible for all three duties – calling penalties, offsides, and icings. As a result, when they try to get up ice to call the offside they frequently miss what is going on behind them. On top of it all, if one of the refs started the game by making a lot of calls, the other referee might try to assert himself by making more calls. There was a risk of there being a conflict between the two and the game would suffer. That problem did not exist in the NHL."

"Did Sinden get the Soviets to agree to change the officiating system?"

"Nope. The Soviet authorities wouldn't budge. And when it came to picking the actual on-ice officials, Sinden and his colleagues were not bothered with their identities and the Soviets ended up picking the eight referees that would be used in the series and the Canadians agreed to them. For the Canadian games, the officials would be four Americans, Gordon Lee, Len Gagnon, Frank Larson, and Steve Dowling. Sinden did not know it at the time, but the Soviets had had a record of success in international play with Lee and Gagnon working their games. The four referees who would work the games in Moscow were the two West Germans, Franz Baader and Josef Kompalla, a Swede, Uwe Dahlberg, and a Czechoslovak, Rudolf (Rudy) Bata.

The Canadians and the Soviets further agreed to a formula to determine which referees would officiate which games in Canada and Moscow. In both countries, the four referees would be lettered A, B, C, and D. A and B would work the first game and then C and D would work the next game. The Canadians and the Soviets agreed that after the first two games, they would hold a conference to pick the officials for games 3 and 4. Both sides would try to cooperate on who they thought were the best two of the four who had worked. If they couldn't agree, then in Canada the Canadians would choose the officials for game 3, and the Soviets would choose the officials for game 4. The same format would be used in Moscow."

"That seems fair but sounds complicated."

"The arrangement was fair and it sounded like the officiating issue was resolved, but it would later turn out to be a major headache for Sinden and Team Canada. Regarding the scouting, it was agreed that each team would have some scouts who would check out the other team before the series began and report back to their team about what they saw so they could be better prepared. It was agreed that Canada would send two scouts to Moscow to watch the Soviet team, and the Soviets would send a couple of scouts to Canada. Once Sinden and Ferguson were back in Canada what do you think the team did to get ready before the series started?"

"Get together and practice!" Andy responded.

"Right! The first game of the series was going to be on September 2. Team Canada's training camp started on August 13. That gave them less than three weeks to prepare for what became the biggest hockey event in Canadian history. The coaches tried their best to help the team prepare itself for the series but they had some attitude problems to deal with. Articles in the media suggested the Canadians would easily win the series and many sportswriters expressed the opinion that Canada would sweep the series with eight lopsided wins. Although the coaches knew the Soviets had a strong team and that beating them would not be easy, the overly optimistic predictions in the media made the players believe that their victory in the series was practically guaranteed. Then there was something else that added to this overconfidence."

"What was that?"

"The scouting report! The very thing that was supposed to provide the Canadian team with a reality check ended up doing the opposite by providing a false picture. Two experienced Canadian scouts went to the Soviet Union for six days. They watched a couple of games in which some of the players were on the national team and only saw the national team goalie, Vladislav Tretiak, play in one game. His team was defeated 8–1. The scouts only had an opportunity to see the entire Soviet national team together at one practice session. Based on what they saw, the scouts reported that the Soviets were weak and the Canadians would not have any trouble beating the Soviets. The Canadians could have made a better effort to learn about their opponents by studying the recent Soviet performances at the Olympics and World Championships. I have no idea why they didn't."

"What about the Soviet scouts? Did they get a false impression of Team Canada too?"

"No siree! The Soviets took the whole matter of studying the Canadian team very seriously. The Soviets had already compiled extensive files on every Canadian player and knew everything about them. They watched films of the recent NHL playoffs. They also sent several coaches to Canada to watch every Team Canada training session from the stands. They took endless pages of notes about what the Canadians were doing. The Soviets had a very good idea of what to expect from Team Canada. However, besides the general overconfident attitude that the Canadian players had, there was another problem".

"What problem was that?" Andy asked.

"Hockey is a team sport and developing team chemistry does not just happen when the players put on the same jersey. Back in those days, there was not much, if any, fraternizing with the players on other teams. Throughout the season players stuck to their teams and they didn't particularly like the guys on the other teams. The intensity of the hostility rose during the playoffs. Many of the guys on Team Canada who had played against each other just months ago during the Stanley Cup finals disliked each other. Spending time together after practices would help the players from different teams to get to know each other, but that would take time. Most teams usually have to go through some challenging experience together, like a tournament, before they come together and play as a unit. Team Canada did not have much time.

As Team Canada prepared themselves many Canadians assumed that they were doing what needed to be done to get themselves in top shape and ready to do their best against the Soviets. The media hype about the Summit Series intensified in August. It all added to a building sense of excitement and anticipation. It was as though the country was swept up in an epidemic of hockey fever and the temperature kept going up and up. When I heard sportswriters and commentators saying that Canada was going to handily win the series, I felt a degree of relief and comfort. I hoped they were right. However, my father told me several times that those commentators were simply naïve and overconfident. He instilled in me a nagging feeling that something was wrong and he explained why."

"Why? What was it that was wrong?"

"As you know, my father was a history professor. He specialized in North American history, but he knew a lot about European history, and that included Russian and Soviet history. He was sure that the Soviets would not have agreed to the series if they did not feel confident that they would win. Canada was an open society and my father was certain that the Soviets had used all the resources at their disposal to study the NHL and all the Canadian players. He was sure that the Soviets had already conceived of game plans that would neutralize Team Canada's strengths and exploit its weaknesses. My father suspected the Canadian hockey officials knew little about the Soviet team and had no idea what they had gotten themselves into. He thought the Canadians were in for a big surprise. This was not going to be a cakewalk but one hell of a fight.

One of the things my father explained to me was that the Soviet government would dedicate whatever resources were necessary to any endeavour that they considered a priority. The Soviets may not always succeed in achieving their objective but they were keen on proving themselves, and their communist system, as being the best at everything. Athletics was one area where they did everything to develop their best athletes so they could win international competitions and boast that the communist system was the best. Thus, my father told me that this was not just going to be a series of exhibition hockey games. One had to consider the series in the context of the Cold War between the Eastern communist bloc and the Western free world. There was a war going on in Vietnam and the communists were on the other side. Both teams represented their respective countries, including the political and economic systems and corresponding values. The series wasn't just about hockey. The way my father explained it to me, Canadians were lucky to live in a free society while the Soviets lived in a dictatorship. The Soviet economy never lived up to its potential and they had few human rights as we understood them. The Soviet players who wore the Soviet uniform represented the communist system. The Canadian players represented our liberal democracy. To my father, me, and many other Canadians, it was clear who were the good guys and the bad guys. In my mind, Canada had to win. It simply had to."

Andy and his grandfather had been paddling around the lake and were about halfway around. As the morning sun climbed in the sky the temperature rose and was expected to be hot by noon.

"Okay, Andy. So what I just told you was some of the background that helps explain how the series came about and the context. Let's take a break from all the paddling and let the canoe drift for a while so we can drink some water and have a snack. After we start paddling again, I'll tell you what happened in the games in Canada."

"OK, Gramps," Andy said as he swung around in his seat to face his grandfather and reached for his water bottle and a granola bar.

CHAPTER 3:
GAME 1 IN MONTREAL

Once Andy and Floyd finished their snack break Andy turned around on his seat and they both resumed paddling. "Now that you know what happened before the series, let's get on with the games!"

"All right!" Andy said as he imagined himself in the stands watching a game.

"The first game in the series was held in the Montreal Forum on Saturday, September 2, 1972. It was the last long weekend of the summer as Monday would be Labour Day and a holiday. The second game in the series would take place on Monday in Toronto. School would start on Tuesday. By that time my classmates and I would have two games to talk about!

After months of waiting the day had finally arrived. There was so much tension in the air you could feel it. All day long on that Saturday, I was excited and at the same time, I was nervous. Sinden had a large roster of players to pick from. However, he could only dress 19 players for each game so he picked his players for the first game based on their performance during the training camp and set up some forward lines and defensive pairings. Sinden decided to have a dozen forwards which would be four lines, and five defencemen. The other two players would be the goalie and his backup. Having five defencemen was common in NHL games, however, being on the ice every second shift or so was easier when the players were in mid-season form. Guess who was in nets?"

"Ken Dryden!" Andy replied excitingly.

"Good guess! Sinden had three goalies to pick from and his original plan was that Dryden would play in the first game since he would likely get a lot of support from the Montreal crowd. Tony Esposito was slated to play in the second game. Whichever of them played better would then play in the third game. If things worked out as hoped and the Canadians were winning all the games, Ed Johnston would play in the fourth game."

"Why did the coach want to change goalies all the time, Gramps?"

"Sinden thought that the pressure of playing in consecutive games in this series would be too much for one goalie. He thought it would be better for the goalies to take turns so they would be able to fully rest after their games and be in peak mental shape for their next game. For the forward lines, Sinden picked a couple of player combinations. One was Bobby Clarke, Paul Henderson, and Ron Ellis. Another was Phil Esposito, Frank Mahovlich, and Yvan Cournoyer. The third one was the Rangers' GAG line of Jean Ratelle, Vic Hadfield, and Rod Gilbert. A final line was Red Berenson, Mickey Redmond, and Pete Mahovlich. On defence, Don Awrey was paired with Rod Seiling and Brad Park played with Gary Bergman. The fifth defenceman was Guy Lapointe."

"Who was on the Soviet team?"

"Good question. Back then no Soviet player played in the NHL. The Soviet players were largely unknown to the Canadian public. However, it would not take long for some of the Soviet players to make themselves known. By the end of the series Canadian hockey fans would be familiar with the names of the Soviet players. I did not know any of the Soviet players' names when the series started but there were three names that I heard during that first game that I never forgot. Two were their star forwards, Alexander Yakushev and Valeri Kharlamov. Yakushev was over six feet tall and Kharlamov was about five foot nine inches. Both made huge impressions when they were on the ice. But the biggest surprise was their twenty-year-old goalie Vladislav Tretiak. He turned out to be outstanding."

"Did the Soviets rotate their goalies too?"

"No, they didn't. The Soviets used the same goalie in every game of the series. Although Tretiak was young the Soviet coaches had a lot of confidence in him because he was so good. So, what do you think Sinden's game plan was?"

"Score a lot of goals and win the game!" Andy said laughingly.

"Yeah, that's a good game plan for every game, but he had some specific instructions for his players in this game. He wanted them to put as much offensive pressure on the Soviets as possible; play the same style of hockey that they played in the NHL; shoot as much as they could at the net and from any angle because they thought the goalie was poor; to be aggressive, but only when they were in a position to hit; and to avoid any fighting. The coaches thought that if the Canadian players were aggressive enough, they might score a couple of quick goals and make the Soviets panic and then the Canadians would take advantage of any Soviet mistakes and score more goals."

"That sounds like a good game plan."

"It sure sounded good, but the coaches had no idea of what to expect from the Soviets or how they would react to Team Canada's aggressiveness. Something happened before the game in the Soviet dressing room that showed just how naïve some people, including veteran hockey players, were about the strength of the Soviet team. Have you ever heard of Jacques Plante?"

"No. Who was he?" Andy asked.

"Plante was the NHL goalie who created the first goalie mask. He was sure the Soviets would be soundly beaten in the game and the series. As a goaltender, he felt a degree of solidarity with the Soviet goalie and before the game, he went to see Tretiak in the Soviet dressing room. Plante was known to the Soviets. They let him in and he told Tretiak what to expect from some of the Canadian sharpshooters like Phil Esposito and Yvan Cournoyer and gave him some tips about how to deal with their shots. Can you believe that?"

"That was a nice thing to do though, wasn't it?" Andy suggested.

"Sure, it was a nice thing to do but Plante could have saved his breath. All of Canada would soon find out how good Tretiak was and that he didn't need any tips from Plante or anyone else. Do you think any Soviet veteran came by to give the Canadian goalie some tips on what to expect from the Soviet players and how to effectively deal with them?"

"No."

"Instead, the Soviet coaches showed how they would try to gain even the smallest advantage in their favour."

"What do you mean, Gramps?"

"Standard procedure was for the official score record keeper to go to both team dressing rooms before the game to ask for the team lineup list. The visitors were supposed to provide the official with their lineup first and the home team second. The Soviets were the visitors and the Canadians were the home team. Sinden was particularly interested in finding out who would be in the Soviet lineup because he wanted to set up the Ellis-Clarke-Henderson line against the line that Valeri Kharlamov would play on. What do you think the Soviets did when the official asked them for their lineup?

"What?"

"They refused to give it to him and insisted that the Canadians provide their lineup first. Sinden stuck to his guns and the official had to go back and deal with the Soviets who gave him a hard time. Sinden did not want to give in because he was concerned that the Soviets might think they could get away with anything. Eventually, the Soviets coughed it up. Sinden found out that the Kharlamov line wasn't going to start the game. That's all he wanted to know and he assigned Phil Esposito's line to start the game.

That evening at home I sat with my father to watch the game on the television. My mother was never interested in hockey so she did not join us. When we turned on the television, we saw that the Forum was full and Prime Minister Pierre Elliott Trudeau was there and my father was pleasantly surprised by a familiar sound."

"What was that?"

"The voice of legendary hockey broadcaster Foster Hewitt! The NHL games were first broadcast on radio and then on television. Foster Hewitt was a former hockey broadcaster who called the Toronto Maple Leafs games on radio and television for years. Hewitt coined the expression 'He shoots, he scores!' He stopped calling games in the 1960s but came out of retirement to broadcast the Summit Series games along with another sportscaster named Brian Conacher who happened to be a former NHL player. Hewitt's return further reinforced the feeling that this hockey series was a big deal. How many people do you think watched the game?"

"I don't know. Maybe five million?"

"Out of 22 million Canadians, it was estimated that 12 million Canadians watched the first game. Tens of millions more would see it in the Soviet Union and elsewhere."

"Whoa! That's a lot of people!"

"It sure was. All my friends were probably watching the game. When the teams came out on the ice there was a striking difference in appearance between the two teams. Team Canada's jersey was red on top with the shape of the maple leaf on the bottom half of the front in white. Their pants were black. The maple leaf emblem was not just a small leaf patch like the one on the Toronto Maple Leafs jersey but a huge one that took up the bottom half of the jersey in the front. 'Canada' was written on the back. I thought the Canadian uniform was beautiful and exciting."

"What was the Soviet uniform like?"

"The Soviet uniform was a bland white jersey with the letters 'CCCP' across the front. Their pants were red. I remember looking at the Soviet players as they lined up at their blue line during the opening ceremony and when I saw the letters CCCP it was clear that those hockey players represented the Soviet communist system."

"What did CCCP stand for?" Andy asked.

"That was the Russian abbreviation for USSR. The other thing that was striking about the contrast between the two teams was that all the Soviets wore the same red helmets while only three Canadians wore a helmet."

"Who were they?"

"Paul Henderson, Gordon Berenson, and Stan Mikita. Without their helmets, it was easier to identify the players on Team Canada. Bergman was easy to identify because he was bald! Before the start of the first game, there was a ceremonial faceoff with the Prime Minister dropping the puck. Even though it was just a ceremonial event that did not have any consequence, Phil Esposito was determined to win the faceoff and he did which contributed to the tremendous excitement and anticipation among Canadian fans. The two referees were Gordon Lee and Len Gagnon. Although Phil Esposito won the ceremonial faceoff, he lost the first one at the start of the game. But it did not take him long to make his presence felt. Bergman got the puck and made a pass to Esposito. He and his linemates Cournoyer and Frank Mahovlich drove to the net and Mahovlich shot a backhander that Tretiak kicked out. Esposito got in front of the net and batted the puck in the air and it went into the net. It only took thirty seconds for Team Canada to score and we were up 1-0!"

"Holy smokes! That was fast!"

"Yup! It sure was. The crowd at the Forum erupted in cheers and celebration. I felt like an electric shock jolted me out of my seat to join in the celebration! My father was also pleasantly surprised and clapped his hands. If Team Canada could score that quickly many people thought it would probably score a lot more before the game was over."

"All right! Great start to the game!"

"By the way, every time that I tell you the score in a game the first number will always be Canada's score and the second number will be the Soviet score. So 1-0 means Canada is up by a goal. I always find it confusing when announcers say at one moment that a team is up 1-0 and later down 2-1. Which number represents which team?"

"Okay. I get it. The first number is the Canadian score and the second is the Soviet one. Right," Andy said.

"About six minutes later Team Canada did it again. There was a faceoff in the Soviet end that Clarke won. Henderson was at the top of the faceoff circle and he one-timed it into the corner of the Soviet net. Suddenly it was 2-0 and the game was only six and a half minutes old. The crowd at the Forum erupted in cheers again and my father and I were having a great time. Many Canadians thought that the game was unfolding according to the predictions and a Canadian victory was in the bag. Things were going well, right?"

"Sure sounds like it!"

"Well, not quite. The Soviets did not panic. They were composed and didn't flinch. Despite the two goals, the Soviets were tearing up and down the ice making sharp passes and outskating the Canadians to the puck. It did not take long to realize that the Soviet players were in top physical condition. About five minutes later the Soviets put on pressure in the Canadian zone and passed the puck back and forth while the Canadians skated around trying unsuccessfully to chase the puck down. Eventually, the puck got to Yevgeni Zimin who was alone on the left side of the net. He fired it up high and the Soviets scored their first goal at 11:40. Suddenly it was 2-1. At that point, my father stopped smiling and looked increasingly worried. A little later the Soviets got a penalty and the Canadians came close but couldn't score on the power play. The Soviets did a good job of killing their penalty and when the penalty was over they got another penalty at 17:19 of the period."

"Great! Did the Canadians score this time?"

"That would have been a great opportunity for the Canadians to get a power play goal and restore their two-goal lead before the end of the first period. Instead, nine seconds into the Soviet penalty the Soviets won the faceoff in their end and took it up the ice and Vladimir Petrov scored a short-handed goal. The first period ended tied 2-2."

"Oh, oh!" Andy mumbled.

"So the game started with two quick Canadian goals and everyone feeling great but by the first intermission the game was tied and Canadian fans were concerned. The Soviet team was good and seemed to have their act together better than the Canadian one. Still, there were forty minutes to go and that was plenty of time for Team Canada to get back on top.

Then the second period started. At the 2:40 mark of the second period, Kharlamov got the puck on the right side of the rink and skated up the wing. Kharlamov proved himself to be a very skilled opponent. He deked a Canadian defenceman and skated around the player from the outside with one hand on his stick while protecting the puck. He then cut straight to the goal and managed to bring the puck to his forehand pulling a fake on Dryden and shooting it in the five hole. It was an impressive display of skill and agility. That kind of move was not that common in the NHL."

"Oh, wow," Andy exclaimed.

"Oh, wow, is right. A lot of people didn't expect that kind of play and skill from the Soviets. That goal was a real wake-up call for those who needed a reality check. The second period is not starting well as the Canadians were now down 2-3."

"Gramps, where did that expression 'five hole' come from? I know it is the space between the goalie's legs, but why call it that? I never hear the coaches talk about first or second holes," Andy asked.

"When a goalie is in the standard ready position in the nets there are five open spaces that a shooter can shoot at. The four corners at the top and bottom of the net are the first four holes. The fifth hole is the space between the goalie's legs when his skates are spread. Saying that a goal was scored in the five hole is a simple way of saying that the puck went between the goalie's legs."

"Ok, I get it."

"Kharlamov was not finished. He put on a show in the second period and halfway through the period he took a slapshot from the top of a faceoff circle and scored again. By the end of the second period, the Soviets had scored four straight goals and were now leading 2-4. Things were not looking good."

"Did the Canadians try anything to stop Kharlamov, Gramps?"

"Once Kharlamov was recognized as the threat that he was Sinden assigned Ron Ellis to cover him. Ellis had his hands full for the rest of the series. What compounded the discomfort over the score was that it seemed that the Canadian players were out of breath and getting sluggish while the Soviets were hustling on the ice like a well-oiled machine and weren't even breaking a sweat. The Canadians just couldn't keep up. By then the game had also made the contrasting styles of the two teams glaringly obvious. While the Soviets were all about puck control and passing back and forth until they got a good shot on the net the Canadians were running around and getting beaten to loose pucks every time. Whatever nervous energy Team Canada had at the beginning of the game quickly disappeared as they tired themselves out and demonstrated how out of shape they were compared to the Soviets. In his 1989 memoir, Ferguson wrote that our guys were running all over the place and every player seemed to be trying to do the other player's job. The team was not playing solid, positional hockey. Unfortunately, the Soviet style thrived on other players being out of position.

Normally when I watched an NHL game on Saturday night with my father I would typically go to bed after the second period. Sometimes I would be allowed to stay up and watch the third period if it was an exciting game between the Canadiens and the Bruins or a playoff game. For this series, I stayed up and watched the games in their entirety."

"So how did the third period go? Did the Canadians get back into the game?"

"Just after the eight-minute mark in the third period Henderson passed to Ellis on the right side in the Soviet zone and he one-timed it towards the Soviet goal where Clarke deflected it into the net. That made it 3-4."

"Great! Canada was catching up!" Andy interjected excitingly.

"Yup, and a lot of people were hoping that Team Canada would pour it on and tie the game soon and then get the lead back. About five minutes after Canada's third goal Cournoyer took a shot that hit the post. That could have tied up the game, but instead, it bounced away. Then the Soviets got possession and Yuri Blinov passed to Boris Mikhailov who scored with a backhand shot. The Soviets restored their two-goal lead and the score was now 3-5. That was a real turning point in the game."

"Aww..." Andy moaned.

"There were just over six minutes left in the game and Team Canada would have to score three goals to win. Instead, less than a minute later Zimin scored his second goal of the game to make the score 3-6. At that point, it was obvious that Team Canada was going to lose. I hoped they would score, but instead, with just a minute and a half left in the game, Yakushev scored another Soviet goal. The final score was 3-7. If that humiliating loss was not bad enough, an unfortunate incident right after the final buzzer added to the embarrassment."

"What happened?"

"There was a screw-up with the ritual at the end of the game. In the NHL the teams normally head straight to their dressing rooms. The only time you see teams line up for handshakes after a game is at the end of a playoff series. However, in international matches, the tradition was that the teams line up after every game for handshakes."

"So what happened?"

"The Canadian team was unaware of the handshake protocol and went to their dressing room while the Soviets lined up expecting to shake hands. The Soviets probably thought that the disappearing Canadians were a bunch of sore losers. Alan Eagleson was in the stands and saw what was happening and rushed to the Canadian dressing room to get the Canadians back on the ice. However, by the time they returned, the Soviets had already left. No one had told the coaching staff about this protocol after every game but they should have been aware of international rules and customs. The Canadians ended up apologizing to both the Soviet team and the crowd that was still in the stands."

"Did they apologize to the crowd for losing the game too?" Andy asked sarcastically. He could be a witty and mischievous kid sometimes.

"Ha, ha. Very funny. No, but instead of going back to the dressing room and having a talk with the players the Canadian coach attended a post-game press conference and talked about how good the Soviets were. He admitted that the Canadians were beaten in every facet of the game. The game was a disaster and the final result was a terrible disappointment. I felt stunned and unable to say anything afterward. I wanted to go to bed and sleep but I was too disturbed to unwind and relax. What the heck happened? It was supposed to be our game!

My father's assessment was that the Canadians skated around with no cohesion as though they were at a local rink playing some sort of pick-up game of shiny hockey while the Soviets were composed and played like robots that steamrolled the Canadians. My father told me that it seemed like the Soviets were thoroughly prepared to play against Team Canada but the Canadians were nowhere near ready to play the Soviets. He was disappointed because he knew that the Canadians could have played a lot better. However, he remained stoical as he reminded me that there were seven more games in the series and the Canadians now had a pretty good idea of what they were up against. They would either step up to overcome the challenge or reveal themselves to be the inferior hockey players. It was as though my worst fears were coming true and the rest of the country was in the same state of shock as I was. I was in a sad and pensive mood the next morning. However, the newspapers would not carry critical headlines about the game until the Monday morning papers so Canadian hockey fans would thus experience two depressing mornings in a row."

"Is that what happened?" Andy asked.

"That's exactly what happened! The news stories described a defeat that was a national shame. I felt sorry for the Canadian hockey players and hoped they would not give up. All day long on Sunday and Monday I ruminated about what had happened in that first game and went through all the possible explanations for the Canadian failure while trying to convince myself that these were not just cop-out excuses."

"Like what explanations, Gramps?" Andy asked.

"There were lots of factors starting with the timing of the series. It was at the worst time of the year and guaranteed that our players would be in lousy shape. The Soviet players were in peak physical condition while our guys couldn't keep up and were out of gas by the third period. While the Canadian training camp had started on August 13, the Soviet National Team gathered on July 5 to prepare for the series. The Canadian training camp should have started earlier or the series should have been after the playoffs."

"Anything else?"

"Well, hockey is a team sport. There was an obvious lack of cohesiveness and coordination during that first game. The players were from different NHL teams and had no experience playing together. While the Soviet National Team had already played in the World Championships earlier that year, this was Team Canada's first game! And there was more."

"Like what?"

"I kept thinking that Team Canada was not really composed of Canada's best players and the two best players were missing."

"Who were they?"

"The two Bobbys."

"Who?"

"Bobby Hull and Bobby Orr. Bobby Hull had played for Chicago and had the hardest slapshot in the league."

"Why didn't he play?"

"That year a new hockey league called the World Hockey Association [WHA] had been created to rival the NHL. The WHA tried to create teams in some American cities that had no hockey teams as well as in some smaller Canadian cities. They also tried to get some of the known NHL players who had a lot of fans to switch leagues. The new team in Winnipeg signed Bobby Hull that year with the largest hockey contract in history to that time. A million bucks in those days was a heck of a lot of money. The problem was that the NHL sanctioned the series and insisted that only players with an NHL contract were allowed to play. No WHA players were allowed to play. In that sense, Team Canada was not really Team Canada but Team NHL."

"What about the other Bobby? He was invited to be on the team."

"Bobby Orr had just had surgery on his left knee in June that year. He tried to skate with Team Canada during practice but his knee had not yet healed and it swelled up. That made it impossible for him to play in the series. Bobby Orr ended up joining the team's entourage and traveled with the team to Moscow, but he didn't play in any games. His absence on the ice, and that of Bobby Hull, were huge gaps in Team Canada's lineup. Many people believed that had Bobby Hull played we would have scored more goals and that had Bobby Orr played the Soviets would not have scored as many as they did. But there was more!"

"Now what?"

"Another problem for the team had to do with the lack of information that Team Canada had about the Soviets before the series started. This is one of the life lessons to come out of the series. Always keep this in mind... whenever you are in a struggle against an opponent, getting as much information about the opposition in advance is helpful. The more you have, the better. It's the same thing in the military where such information about the enemy is called 'intelligence.' Generals who have lots of accurate intelligence about the opponent's size, positions, weapons, plans, strategy, and tactics are in a much better position to deal with the enemy than generals who have no information about the enemy and might fall into a trap and get ambushed. A Chinese philosopher ages ago named Sun Tsu wrote a book titled *The Art of War* in which he said that when you are strong you should show that you are weak and when you are weak you should show that you are strong."

"Why?"

"Because that kind of deception may prompt your opponent to make the wrong decisions and give you a better chance of winning. The fact is that the Soviets were masters of deception and the Canadians should not have been taken by surprise. Perhaps if they had known more about the Soviet national team, they might have been better prepared."

"I see. So did you think that if the Canadians lost the series, it would be because of these problems from the beginning?"

"I didn't know what to think. I was confused and just trying to understand what was going on. But not everything was gloomy."

"What do you mean, Gramps?"

"Ironically, there was a silver lining to the loss. In a way, the loss proved to have had a beneficial effect. This is another important life lesson that you should know if you don't already."

"What's that?" Andy asked.

"It's this: if you take a positive approach and review the mistakes that you made in a loss and figure out how to correct the situation, you will likely learn a lot more than if you had won. The best learning and improvement often come after a defeat. People who win all the time have no incentive to reevaluate and change to improve. Why improve when you are already the winner, right?"

"Yeah, I guess," Andy responded.

"Well, that loss called for some serious analysis and reflection on what happened in Game 1. The Canadian coaches and players had to figure out how to counter the Soviet strengths and exploit whatever weaknesses they could find in the Soviet game. They also needed to figure out how to make fewer mistakes and score more goals in the coming games. One thing was for sure... the Soviets made it clear that they were not amateurs. Nobody in Canada believed that anymore."

"Hey, Gramps, how do you remember all this stuff?" Andy asked.

"Well, I was old enough to understand a lot of what was going on and I remember much of what happened. The Summit Series was such an important and dramatic event that it consumed me throughout the entire month of September 1972 and I've regularly thought about it since. I couldn't forget it. On top of it all, right after the series a couple of books came out and my mother got one for me. It was a French book titled *Le match du siècle* that described each game and provided all the statistics for the series. It also had a lot of photographs from each game. I looked at that book every day for about a month before I eventually put it away and did not look at it again for a long time. Over the years several other books about the series came out, especially around anniversaries, and I would eventually buy some of them and add them to my collection. I also bought some of the VHS documentary videos about the series that came out later as well as the collections of the games on DVDs. It was a sort of nostalgia thing for me. But every book or video or DVD got me increasingly interested in finding out the full story of the Summit Series. Over the years, the more I read, the more I became fascinated with the details of what happened on and off the ice. Eventually, I felt I knew the key elements of the story by heart. One thing I can say without hesitation is that the more I learned about the history of the Summit Series the more I considered Team Canada to be even better than I had previously thought."

"What was your favourite book on the series?"

"Oh, that's a good question. There are several. First, both Sinden and Dryden kept a diary during the series and published books about the series immediately after. Harry Sinden's book is called *Hockey Showdown: The Canada-Russia Hockey Series*. Sinden's is probably my favourite book on the series because he described a lot of his thinking at different stages of the series and what happened behind the scenes that the public did not know. Sinden didn't sugarcoat anything and wrote with sincerity.

Ken Dryden's book titled *Face-Off at the Summit* is informative and provides Dryden's unique perspective as a Team Canada member who played in some games and watched others from the stands. Dryden just wrote another book about the series called *The Series: What I Remember, What it Felt Like, What it Feels Like Now*.

Paul Henderson wrote a couple of wonderful books about his life and the impact of having scored the most famous goal in Canadian history. One was called *Shooting for Glory* and the other was *The Goal of My Life: A Memoir*. John Ferguson and several players on the team also wrote hockey memoirs that contain a chapter or two about the series that are informative. Ferguson's book and Phil Esposito's book both have the same title: *Thunder and Lightning*. However, there is a difference between them when it comes to the subtitles."

"What's the difference?"

"Ferguson's book has no subtitle while Esposito's is *A No-B.S. Hockey Memoir*."

"Ha, ha!"

"There were also books by some key people who helped organize and manage the series. One was by Alan Eagleson titled *Power Play: The Memoirs of Hockey Czar Alan Eagleson*. The other was by a Canadian diplomat named Gary J. Smith who wrote *Ice War Diplomat: Hockey Meets Cold War Politics at the 1972 Summit Series*. There were also books by sports journalists and historians that were either specifically about the series or about the historic hockey rivalry over the decades between Canada and Russia. And every time that you think that the last word had been published, it does not take long for another book with a different perspective to come out. I've tried to collect as many as I could. I don't have every book that was published about the series, but I have a lot of them. So the story I'm telling you is a combination of what I remember and what I subsequently read or saw on the TV screen when I watched the games and related documentaries."

"Do you have any Soviet books about the series? Were any Soviet books translated into English?"

"Great question, Andy! Good for you! Here's another life lesson that you should know. Whenever reading history it is always important to recognize that there are often two or more sides to any story. Acquiring an accurate understanding of history often requires reading many different interpretations from different sources. I don't speak or read Russian. However, I read some books by Canadian authors about the history of Soviet hockey that elaborate on the Soviet perspective on the series. I also read one book by the Soviet goalie that was translated into English."

"Really? What was that like?"

"It was a disappointment! Tretiak's book *Tretiak: The Legend* came out in 1987. Many years later I picked up a used copy at a thrift store. When I read it, I found the writing style similar to that of the Soviet political tracts that I had to read during my political science studies at university. It was so boring! I don't know if he actually wrote it or had some Soviet government committee write it for him but when I got to the part where he insisted that he and all his teammates were amateurs I thought he lost credibility and I lost interest in the book.

But there is something else related to your question about getting the other side of the story that I want to tell you. What happens in a free country like Canada is that any time something important occurs people express their opinions. Public opinion is often divided and rarely unanimous. The same goes for the Canadian reaction to the Summit Series of 1972. There are lots of books about it that generally tell the same story and describe Team Canada as an outstanding team that provided Canadians with the thrill of a lifetime. However, there are also several books written by Canadians that are critical of Team Canada and the generally accepted Canadian narrative about the series. Some of the critical books also mirror some of the Soviet criticisms of Team Canada."

"I see. Do you have some of these critical books, Gramps?

"Of course! Some of the points they raise are thought-provoking and valid. Just remember to read all books with your eyes wide open. The more you know about a subject and the related facts, the easier it is to assess interpretations or opinions and detect a bias and that may explain a distorted account or a convenient omission. Okay, enough about the history books. More hockey!"

"Yeah! What happened in Game 2?"

CHAPTER 4:
GAME 2 IN TORONTO

"The two teams met again at the Maple Leaf Gardens in Toronto on Labour Day, Monday, September 4, for the second game of the series."

"The where?" Andy asked.

"The Maple Leaf Gardens was the arena where the Toronto Maple Leafs played at the time. The arena was one of Canada's hockey shrines along with the Montreal Forum. Both arenas served their purposes well for decades, only to be replaced by newer, bigger, better, and more modern facilities. The referees for this game were Frank Larsen and Steve Dowling. Larsen had experience refereeing international games. However, Dowling was the youngest of the refs designated to officiate the games in Canada. His experience was mostly limited to officiating American Hockey League games.

It was crucial for Team Canada to win the second game. If they lost, we would be down by two games, and getting out of the hole would be difficult. They simply couldn't afford to lose this one. The suspense and anticipation that built up before the second game was just as intense as before the first game but with the difference that we all now knew what the Soviets could do. The uncertainty was whether Team Canada would be able to play a more effective game than they did in Game 1.

The Canadians needed to make some adjustments to their game plan and lineup. Fortunately, Sinden and Ferguson were on the ball and made the necessary changes."

"What did they change?" Andy asked.

"The first game was more of a wide-open game focused on offence. The game plan in the second game was to tighten things up and play more of a physical game. On offence, the plan was to forecheck smarter and harder to regain possession of the puck in the Soviet's zone. Before Game 1 the Canadians thought that their speed and quickness would help them beat the Soviets. Instead, the Soviets showed that they were faster. The strategy in the second game was to slow the Soviets down. On defence, it was to pay more attention to detail and backcheck in the Canadians' zone with greater intensity and force the Soviets to shoot from the outside. The idea was to play an NHL-style physical game that the Canadians were used to but the Soviets weren't."

"Did the coach make any changes to the lineup?"

"Sinden also made a lot of changes to the lineup. First, Tony Esposito was in nets and Ed Johnston served as the backup goalie. Some guys were taken out because they did not play that well. The Soviets were remarkably quick in their transition game from defence to offence and anyone who could not keep up with them would have to be replaced. Up front, the Rangers' GAG line of Ratelle, Hadfield, and Gilbert was taken out. Red Berenson and Mickey Redmond were also benched. Stan Mikita, Wayne Cashman, J.-P. Parisé, and Bill Goldsworthy got their chance to play. The latter players were known as consistent grinders, especially in the corners, and would likely slow the Soviets down. Sinden decided to strengthen the defence and increase the squad from five to six. Awrey and Seiling were benched while Pat Stapleton, Bill White, and Serge Savard were inserted in the squad."

"Did the Soviets make any changes to their game plan and lineup?" Andy asked.

"After the first game, the Soviet coaches must have assumed that they had the winning formula and did not need to change anything. The Soviets only made two changes to their lineup for the game. The Soviets also had a pretty good idea of what the Canadians intended to do. Although Sinden had wanted his team's practice before the game to be closed, just after it was finished, he noticed that the Soviet coaches were sitting at the top of the stands. They saw everything Team Canada had worked on during their practice. However, the Soviets didn't make any adjustments to their team's strategy and game plan.

As was the case with the Saturday game, I watched Game 2 at home with my father and remember being anxious. When the game started it was clear that Team Canada had something to prove. The players were focused and played with their eyes wide open and their elbows up, just like in the NHL. In the first period, the Canadians got two penalties. However, the Soviets did not capitalize on the power plays, and the first period ended without any goals.

In the second period, there was an instance where Phil Esposito's shadow, a Soviet player called Vladimir Petrov, got a penalty and the referee's arm went up. At that moment Tony Esposito rushed from his goal to the bench so the Canadians could get a sixth attacker on the ice. In the ensuing play, Cashman passed the puck to Phil Esposito who scored at 7:14. Boom! We were up 1-0."

"Yahoo! Way to go Esposito!" Andy said with excitement.

"The game continued with exciting end-to-end action. However, the refs called the game in a manner that was more in the North American style with greater tolerance for physicality. In the last minute of the period, the Soviet player Gennady Tsygankov got a penalty and Kharlamov shoved a referee while arguing with him. He got a ten-minute misconduct penalty for doing that."

"Serves him right," Andy said.

"Kharlamov ended up getting more penalty minutes than anyone else on his team during the series. So at the end of the second period, Team Canada had a one goal lead. That was better than nothing, but one goal was not enough of a margin for comfort. I just prayed that the Canadians would win the game."

"How did the third period go?"

"The third period started with a bang and a beautiful play. Brad Park had the puck in the Canadian zone and broke out to centre. Cournoyer was skating up on the right wing. Park made a perfect pass to Cournoyer on the fly. Cournoyer then outskated the Soviet defenceman on the outside and streaked toward the goal. He fired a shot through the five hole and continued skating behind and around the Soviet net. I was so happy that my favourite player had scored such a beautiful goal! So Canada was up 2-0."

"Cool!" Andy exclaimed.

"The game was turning out to be quite different from the first game. However, there were some similarities. Although the 2-0 lead should have made Canadian fans comfortable and confident, everyone remembered that Canada was up 2-0 in the first game too before the whole thing came crashing down. So guess what happened?"

"The Soviets scored?"

"That's exactly what happened! How did you guess? Four minutes after Cournoyer's goal Bobby Clarke got a penalty. Less than a minute after that Yakushev scored while on the power play. So the score was then 2-1. How do you think the Canadian hockey fans felt?"

"Scared!"

"You better believe it. And then twenty-one seconds later our defenceman Stapleton got a hooking penalty."

"Oh no!"

"Oh no, is right. That's when a lot of people across the country got really apprehensive! The Soviets could have tied the game up while on a power play, but instead, something else happened that was electrifying."

"What?"

"When they were picking players for the team Ferguson wanted Pete Mahovlich on the team because he was good at penalty killing. He sure showed it when it counted. During their power play the Soviets kept up the pressure in the Canadian zone and kept passing the puck around looking for an opening and a chance to score. The four Canadian players maintained their defensive box. There was a faceoff in the Canadian zone and Phil Esposito got the puck and shot it off the boards and out of the Canadians' zone to centre ice where Pete Mahovlich picked it up and had one Soviet defenceman between him and Tretiak. As Mahovlich skated across the Soviet blue line he wound up as though he was going to fire a slapshot. That made the defenceman bring his legs together to block the shot. Mahovlich then pulled a fake and took the puck around the defenceman who was caught flat-footed and headed toward the Soviet goal. Mahovlich then pulled another fake on Tretiak as he moved one way as if to fire a forehand shot. When Tretiak fell to the ice Mahovlich switched to a backhand shot to get the puck in the net. The play finished with the giant Mahovlich falling over Tretiak in the crease but he quickly got up and skated towards the bench with his arms up in celebration. My father and I both yelled 'Yes!' and pumped our arms in the air when we saw the goal. The crowd in the Gardens went nuts. Mahovlich's short-handed goal was an amazing effort that re-established a two goal lead and helped alleviate the fear that the Soviets would tie it up."

55

"Way to go, Pete!" Andy cheered.

"Even though Pete Mahovlich had just scored one heck of a goal, it would prove to be the only goal he scored in the series! However, he made his presence known when he was on the ice, particularly during an incident in Game 8 when he showed what a gutsy guy he was. But we'll get to that later. So the Canadians were then up 3-1 and there were thirteen minutes left in the game. About two minutes later Stan Mikita got the puck and took it behind the Soviet goal. He passed it to Frank Mahovlich at the top of the faceoff circle who shot the puck in the top left corner of the net. The Mahovlich brothers had scored two consecutive goals. Canada was now up 4-1 with eleven minutes left in the game."

"Wow! That's a three-goal lead. The fans must have cheered!"

"They certainly did but caution dictated that everyone save their biggest cheers for when the game was finally over. Fortunately, the Soviets were not able to score any more goals and Canada won 4-1. The series was now tied at one game each."

"Way to go Team Canada!" Andy said excitedly.

"The whole country breathed a sigh of relief. Team Canada had demonstrated that they could make the necessary adjustments and had what it took to beat the Soviets. It seemed like a different team than the one that played two days earlier. They were more disciplined and played with determination. They had played a tighter game with greater control, particularly in their zone where Tony Esposito did a great job in nets. They were also physical, with Cashman, Parisé, and Goldsworthy delivering some thundering bodychecks that were nothing unusual in the NHL. In many ways, it was just another Monday evening at the Gardens or any other NHL arena. As expected, after the game the Canadian players were ecstatic and believed that they had corrected their false start in Game 1 and were on the right track. Even though the Soviets only scored one power play goal, they maintained their team composure throughout the game and never became disorganized.

After each game, the coaches from both teams were expected to participate in and share their thoughts about the games at a press conference. After the first game, Sinden went to the press conference and had to admit that the better team had won that game and left shortly afterward. The Soviet assistant coach said that in the Soviet Union, it was customary for coaches to meet after a sporting event and discuss the game with the press. He then made some negative comments about Sinden whom he thought should have stayed longer. The Soviets seemed to want to gloat and extend the period of discomfort for the Canadian coach as long as possible. However, when the Soviets lost the second game neither the Soviet coach nor any of his assistants bothered to show up at the press conference. Instead, several senior Soviet hockey authorities did something else that was unexpected."

"What did they do?"

"The Soviet officials were so upset at the end of the game that they barged into the referees' dressing room. The Soviets were angry and largely blamed the referees for their loss. The accounts vary a little in some books, but the common thread is that the most senior Soviet hockey official flew into a rage, called the two referees names, and complained about the way they had officiated the game and let the Canadians get away with too much. To emphasize his anger, he kicked a chair over. Some accounts say he kicked several chairs over."

"Oh boy! I guess he was really mad!" said Andy

"He sure was. Can you imagine how the Soviets would have reacted if a Canadian official stormed into the referees' dressing room after a game in Moscow and started knocking furniture over?"

"Did the Canadians try to do that?"

"The Canadians threw some chairs around but it was not in the referees' dressing room. We'll get to that later. Then the Soviets did something else that was also unexpected."

"What'd they do?" Andy asked.

"The Soviet officials met with their Canadian counterparts and insisted on changes to the designated referees for the remaining games in Canada. The Soviets wanted the refs from the first game, Lee and Gagnon, to referee the remaining two games in Canada. In the process, the Soviets told the Canadians that if the Canadians truly wanted to play this series in the spirit of sportsmanship and friendship, they should play the part of the perfect hosts and consent to the Soviet request. Sinden wrote that the Soviets made their request in as nice and pleasant way as they could. At the time the Canadians did not know about the Soviet tantrum in the referees' dressing room."

"Did the Canadians agree to the Soviet request?"

"Yes. The Canadians agreed and naively assumed that should the tables be turned in the Soviet Union the Soviets would reciprocate their willingness to accommodate the visiting team. In the meantime, I was looking forward to starting school the next day and talking with my friends about the series!"

CHAPTER 5:
GAME 3 IN WINNIPEG

"On Tuesday morning I walked the few blocks from the apartment building where I lived with my parents down Van Horne Avenue to Collège Stanislas. My parents spoke a little French and they sent me to a French school so that I would learn the language and become bilingual. The new school year started that day and my new homeroom teacher was Monsieur Daniel Cousineau. He was well-liked by the students at the school and I was looking forward to being in his class.

The biggest thrill on the first day of school every September was meeting my classmates whom I had not seen all summer. At the time Collège Stanislas was a school for boys only and pretty well all my classmates were Montreal Canadiens fans and hockey card collectors. That first day of school we talked a lot about the disappointing loss on Saturday and the exciting victory on Monday. We all expressed similar sentiments and I felt like I was a member of a tribe whose interests and loyalties that month were primarily limited to hockey and Team Canada. The following day we talked about the game scheduled for that evening and our excitement grew with every break.

The third game of the series was on Wednesday, September 6 in Winnipeg. That was the third game in five days. For the Soviets who were in fantastic shape that wasn't a problem. For the Canadians who were in relatively poorer condition, sustaining the required intensity throughout the whole game would be a challenge. As the Soviets requested, the referees for the game were the same who officiated Game 1, Gordon Lee and Len Gagnon.

The Canadians had demonstrated in Game 2 that forechecking and not letting the Soviets break out of their zone with their set plays was crucial if they were to have a chance at winning. The plan for this game was the same. The Canadian coaches made some line changes as they tried to figure out how to improve their team's performance. Originally, Sinden had planned to have the goalies rotate after each game to give them a break and allow them to recover and prepare for their next game. However, after Tony Esposito's outstanding performance in Toronto, he was chosen to play again in the third game.

The Soviet coach made some changes to his team's lineup. Besides making a few changes on defence he inserted three new forwards, Viacheslav Anisin, Yuri Lebedev, and Alexander Bodunov, who had experience playing together and were nicknamed "the Kid Line" because they were young.

That evening my father and I sat in our usual chairs to watch the game on television. I knew my classmates were doing the same with their families and we would have lots to talk about in the morning. Watching the games was turning into a must-see television series for Canadians that took priority over everything else.

The game started with a bang just before the second minute. Bill White took a shot at the Soviet net from the point and it bounced off Tretiak. Parisé got the puck and took a shot and then another one before it went in. Canada was up 1-0 in no time."

"That's the way to do it!" Andy blurted out.

"A minute later the Soviets got a penalty for elbowing. Would the Canadians be able to capitalize and get a two-goal lead in the first couple of minutes?"

"Did they?" Andy asked.

"No. About fourteen seconds into the penalty the Canadians mishandled the puck at their blue line and Vladimir Petrov picked it up and scored a short-handed goal for the Soviets to tie the game up 1-1."

"Aaah, crap!" Andy grumbled.

"During the rest of the period, both goalies did a super job of protecting their nets. Then, with less than two minutes to go in the first period, Bergman fired a pass to Ratelle who passed it to Cournoyer who passed it back to Ratelle who put it in the Soviet net. At the 18:25 mark of the first period Canada was leading 2-1."

"That's better! Way to go, Ratelle!" cheered Andy.

"Then in the fourth minute of the second period, the puck was in a Soviet corner when Cashman got possession and passed it to Phil Esposito who was at home in the slot. Phil one-timed it into the upper right corner. Boom! It's 3-1 for Canada!"

"All right!"

"You know Andy, I sounded like you when I was your age. Every time the Soviets scored it was 'Booo' and every time Canada scored it was 'Hooray!' Then in the eleventh minute of the period, a Soviet player got a tripping penalty. So guess what happened?"

"Did Team Canada score on the power play?" Andy asked.

"Nope. The puck was in a Soviet corner when a Soviet player got it and made a long cross-ice pass to Kharlamov. He skated up the side, past the Canadian defence, skated across the goal mouth, and swept the puck past Tony Esposito into the net. The Soviets had scored two goals so far and they were both short-handed. The Soviets' penalty kill was deadly. But Team Canada was still leading 3-2. Fortunately, less than a minute later White passed the puck to

Clarke who passed it to Henderson and he fired a fifteen-foot shot into the left corner. Canada was up 4-2 at the 13:47 mark of the second period."

"Right on!"

"The game was more than half over and Canada had a two-goal lead. Do you think Canada would be able to hold on?"

"Yes!" Andy said.

"Well, what happened next was a huge disappointment. About a minute after Henderson's goal, Valeri Vasiliev took a shot from the point and Lebedev tipped it in. That made the score 4-3. At that point, there were five minutes left in the second period. Three and a half minutes later the Soviets put pressure in the Canadian zone and passed the puck around until one pass went to Bodunov in front of Tony Esposito and he scored. The score was all tied up at 4-4 a minute and a half before the end of the second period."

"The Canadians lost a two-goal lead! That sucks!"

"Well, that's one way to describe it."

"What happened in the third period?" Andy asked.

"The Canadians ran on empty. It was obvious that the Canadians were done physically. They had nothing left to give and just couldn't get anything going. However, even though the Canadians didn't score any goals, they managed to prevent the Soviets from scoring too. And the Soviets had plenty of chances. Halfway through the period, Cashman got a two-minute minor for slashing. He argued with the referees and then got a ten-minute misconduct penalty which meant that he was finished for the rest of the game. At that point, the Canadians were on the ropes, and the Soviets, with their better conditioning, could have scored a go-ahead goal and finished the Canadians off. But they didn't. They keep passing and passing and when they finally took a shot, they missed the net."

"Good! They screwed-up!"

"At one point Henderson got the puck close enough to the Soviet net that he one-timed a shot and was so sure that it was going in that he even raised his arms to celebrate. Unfortunately, his celebration was premature."

"Why?"

"There was no cause for celebration. Tretiak gloved it before it crossed the line."

"Aww."

"The Canadian scouting report before the series said Tretiak wouldn't be good on high shots and his glove hand was suspect. That turned out to be false. Tretiak's glove hand was just fine. Anyway, it would have been great if that had been a winning goal and the Canadians won the game but no cigar. But guess what Henderson did?"

"What? Did he slam his stick on the ice and get a penalty or something?"

"No! Henderson was so impressed by Tretiak's save that in a gesture of sportsmanship, he skated over and tapped Tretiak on his pads and Tretiak nodded back."

"That was a nice thing for them to do."

"So the game ended in a 4-4 tie. The Canadians had a 3-1 and a 4-2 lead during the game and blew it. However, given how exhausted they looked in the third period, they were lucky to emerge with a tie."

"Why didn't they play overtime or do a shoot-out to determine a winner?" Andy asked.

"The negotiating teams that set the terms for the series in April did not make any provision for overtime periods in the event of a tie. So after three games the series was evenly split with a game apiece and a tie. My father and I were speechless at the end of the game. We were both so disappointed with Team Canada's failure to score a game-winning goal in the third period. I was confused and upset by the whole situation. Why was Team Canada having such a hard time? Why did the Soviets have to be so good? Some of my friends at school were just as perplexed."

"What did your friends say?"

"It was no fun talking with my friends at school. Some of my classmates were more knowledgeable than others but I figured that they just repeated the comments that they heard their parents make. Some guys were optimistic while others concluded that the Canadian players just weren't as good as everyone else thought. I naturally gravitated towards those who were more optimistic and believed that our guys would somehow triumph in the end.

After the first three games and watching the two teams play, the contrast between the two teams' different styles of playing hockey became increasingly clear. The Soviet team was a well-oiled machine that used coordinated set plays, precision passing, and fast skating. They did not shoot at the net until they were close and had an open net. The Soviet players were like trained robots. Sinden wrote after the third game 'Here were these guys who all look the same, skate the same, shoot the same, the whole game without ever changing expression.' Ferguson wrote that after three games the Canadians had learned a lot about the Soviets. Besides the fact that their conditioning was outstanding, they were poised and would remain unfazed even when down by two goals. They just kept playing their style and game until they came back. However, Ferguson also noted that the Soviet players were sneaky and dirty. They tended to 'kick skates' and use their sticks on the Canadian players."

"Kick skates? What did he mean?"

"I think he was referring to slew-footing which is tripping a player by knocking a player's skates out from behind with a kicking or leg-dragging motion. Anyway, after Game 3 the country's anxiety level rose a notch. There was only one game left in Canada and the rest would be in Moscow. If Team Canada was having such a hard time at home, how would they do in Moscow?"

"They'd probably have a harder time over there," Andy mused.

"Exactly. At least, that's what most people thought. The Canadians needed to win the final game in Canada if they were to have a good chance of winning the series. We all waited for the next game. However, I found the tension of waiting made me increasingly more apprehensive. I just prayed that behind the scenes the Canadian players were figuring out what they had to do to defeat the Soviets."

CHAPTER 6:
GAME 4 IN VANCOUVER

"The last game in Canada was in Vancouver on Friday, September 8. It was the fourth game in seven days. After Game 4 there was going to be a break before Game 5 in Moscow during which Team Canada would go to Sweden for some games with the Swedish national team and some team practices.

The referees for Game 4 were again Gordon Lee and Len Gagnon just as the Soviets wanted. Sinden made some line changes and adjustments for the game. After playing in Games 2 and 3 the coach thought it would be best to give Tony Esposito a break. Sinden put Dryden in the nets for Game 4. He assumed that Dryden would be motivated to prove himself better than Tony Esposito and that he would perform better than he had in Game 1.

On the forward lines Wayne Cashman, J.-P. Parisé, Pete Mahovlich, Stan Mikita, and Jean Ratelle were benched. Vic Hadfield, Rod Gilbert, Gilbert Perrault, Dennis Hull, and Bill Goldsworthy were added. On defence, Serge Savard took a hard shot on the ankle during practice after Game 3 and had a hairline fracture. He would be out for a while and would only return to the lineup later in Moscow. Guy Lapointe was also out with an injury. Don Awrey and Rod Seiling replaced them.

All day long in school I looked forward to watching the game that evening with my father. However, as game time approached, I realized that the anxiety I felt during the games spoiled my ability to actually enjoy them. The best hockey players in the world were playing thrilling hockey but I was unable to just sit back and enjoy the show. Sports are supposed to provide entertainment for viewers but this series felt to me like war and Team Canada had met its match. The game did not start well. It was like the team fell off a cliff."

"What happened?" Andy asked.

"Bill Goldsworthy got a cross-checking penalty in the second minute of the game. It only took the Soviets thirty-seven seconds to score a goal. Vladimir Lutchenko took a slapshot from the point that Dryden blocked with his leg pad. However, Boris Mikhailov was there to get the rebound and score. So at the two-minute mark Canada was already down 0–1. Guess what happened next."

"Did Team Canada score?"

"No. The same thing happened all over again! Goldsworthy got another penalty for elbowing at the sixth-minute mark. The Soviets got their second power play. This time it took them a minute and a half to score. Lutchenko took a shot at the net and Mikhailov deflected it in. The same Canadian gets a penalty and the same Soviet player scores. So less than seven and a half minutes into the first period Canada was down 0–2."

"That totally sucks!" Andy blurted out.

"I certainly thought so at the time. When the second period was past the five-minute mark Gilbert Perreault skated from the Canadian end of the rink all the way to the other end and more or less ignored his teammates in a one-man show. He skated past the Soviet net and tried to pass the puck to Frank Mahovlich in the centre but the puck hit the skate of a Soviet defenceman and deflected into the Soviet goal. It was a fluke goal but it still counted. The score was now 1–2."

"Way to go, Perreault!"

"My father and I hoped the Canadians would tie it up soon, but instead, less than a minute after Perreault's goal, the Soviets got a two-on-one which turned into a one-on-none and Yuri Blinov scored at 6:34. The Soviets re-established their two-goal margin and the score was 1–3. Then there was a moment in the second period when it looked like Canada had scored a goal. Hadfield slid a pass in front of the Soviet net and the puck bounced off Gilbert's skate and went in. However, the referee disallowed it."

"Why?" Andy asked.

"He said that Gilbert kicked it in so it didn't count. Sinden said that he did not think the puck was kicked in and that the goal should have counted. That moment was a turning point in the game and the possibility of winning the game increasingly seemed out of reach for the Canadian players. However, later in Moscow, the Canadians would be the beneficiaries in a similar controversial situation when there was a difference of opinion about whether a goal had been scored against Canada. We'll get to that in a couple of games. Later in the period Kharlamov got the puck in the slot and passed it to his teammate Vladimir Vikulov on the right side of the net who one-timed into the corner. The score at the end of the second period was 1–4."

"Sounds like the game was turning into another disaster!"

"It was! And something very unpleasant started happening in the Vancouver arena that got progressively worse during the game."

"What was that?" Andy asked.

"The Canadian crowd in the stands actually started booing Team Canada. It became louder and louder. I remember being disturbed by the crowd's behaviour as I watched the game. The fans in the arena were upset and embarrassed by Team Canada's lousy performance but I could not help wondering whose side they were on. I was just as disappointed as everyone else that Team Canada was not living up to expectations but who boos their own army in the middle of a war?"

"I guess the Vancouver crowd gave up on Team Canada."

"It sure looked that way. But sometimes there is fortune in misfortune."

"What do you mean?"

"All the booing had an impact on the Canadian players. It made them realize they could only count on themselves for support. The booing actually helped in bringing the team together."

"So what happened in the third period, Gramps?"

"In the third period at the two-minute mark, Vladimir Petrov who had been covering Phil Esposito gave him a bear hug from behind and collapsed on top of him. Petrov got a penalty for doing that."

"Good!" Andy blurted out.

"The Canadians didn't score on the power play but they did a few minutes afterward. Just before the seventh minute Goldsworthy had the puck and crossed the blue line. He passed it to Esposito who fired a shot that hit the crossbar and Goldsworthy got there in time to tap in the rebound. That made the score 2-4."

"At least the Canadians scored again," Andy said.

"A little later there was a strange incident that resulted in more booing against Team Canada. Tretiak was out of his net and on his knees while Frank Mahovlich held him down for a long time. It seemed uncharacteristic of Frank Mahovlich to do something like that."

"Why did he do it?"

"I think the incident reflected the frustration that the Canadian players were feeling. It is inconceivable that a Canadian goal would have counted while Mahovlich was sitting on Tretiak so I have no idea what he was thinking. Then at the eleventh minute, the Soviets scored again."

"Oh, no!"

"Yup. This time Yakushev was behind the net and both Bergman and Park were trying to check him when he passed to his teammate Vladimir Shadrin who was all alone in front of Dryden. Dryden stopped the first shot but Shadrin got the rebound and put it in the net. The score was then 2-5 with less than nine minutes left in the game."

"Was that how the game finished?"

"No. With just twenty-two seconds left in the game, Phil Esposito made a nice pass to Dennis Hull who fired a shot past Tretiak to make the final score 3-5."

"Well, at least it wasn't a total blowout."

"It was in a way. Throughout the whole game no matter what the Canadians did on the ice, nothing seemed to work. Despite the three goals, they played an awful game. It seemed like nothing was going right in this series. Sinden later wrote that after watching the Soviets play in four games, he thought their teamwork was amazing because they played every game at the same pace and didn't have any ups and downs. Everything was consistent. The Soviet goalie was surprisingly good and even though he was playing in all the games, none of the pressure seemed to bother him. However, just as everything looked bleak for the Canadians, something happened that was pretty dramatic that touched a lot of Canadians."

"What was that?" Andy asked.

"After every game, there was a ceremony where a player from each team would be recognized as the game star. When the game ended Phil Esposito was named the Canadian game star while Boris Mikhailov was the Soviet game star. After the award ceremony a CTV sports journalist named Johnny Esaw conducted a live television interview with Esposito. On television screens across the country,

Canadians saw and heard Phil Esposito give one of the most inspiring speeches in Canadian sports history. With sweat dripping all over his face Esposito spoke directly to Canadians and told them the players on the team were doing their best and giving it 150% and the booing they got was disappointing and disheartening. He made the case that the only reason the 35 guys on the team came out to play was because they loved their country and for no other reason. Esposito said he doubted the Russian fans would boo their team but if they did, he said he'd come back and apologize. He said everyone had to face the fact that the Soviets had a good team and he didn't think it was fair that the Canadian team should be booed. Esposito's impromptu speech was amazing. His tone and choice of words were perfect."

"Did his speech make a difference, Gramps?"

"That television interview reverberated across the country and went straight to the hearts of many Canadians who saw it. After hearing how Esposito described the overall situation a lot of people felt sympathetic and a renewed urge to support the team. But Team Canada was in a rut and many Canadians were in no mood for speeches. Nonetheless, Phil Esposito was a natural leader who endeared himself to Canadian hockey fans. Ironically, none of his teammates in the dressing room saw it. I loved Esposito's speech but it did not change my mind in any way. I was already 100% behind the team.

So after that last game in Canada, the situation looked pretty grim. The Soviets had two wins, Canada only one, and there was one tie game. The Canadians seemed to have dug themselves into a hole. Team Canada needed to lick its wounds, regroup, and get its act together. Fast. The Moscow games would start in two weeks. One thing for certain. This was no game. It was war on ice and everyone would soon find out whether the Canadian players had what it took to win.

When I went back to school on Monday I spoke with several classmates about the series and how it was evolving. By then the shock of the Friday night loss had abated, but the general mood was gloomy. A few classmates were still optimistic but their positive attitude seemed to ignore the desperate situation that Team Canada was in. Some classmates gave the impression that they thought Team Canada had hit an iceberg and was sinking like the *Titanic*. Some laughed at the Canadian team. Others now ignored the series and moved on to our traditional activity during recess and played dodgeball at one end of the schoolyard.

I still had faith. Despite the break in the series, I could not get it off my mind and kept reflecting on the first four games and wondering what would happen in Moscow. Fortunately, the next stop on Team Canada's itinerary was a useful trip to Sweden which contributed to the team's progression."

CHAPTER 7:
THE STOCKHOLM
INTERLUDE

"After the Vancouver game, the Canadian players dispersed and returned to their homes for a few days. Team Canada reunited in Toronto on September 12 and flew to Stockholm for an eight-day visit. They were scheduled to play two exhibition games with the Swedish national team and hold several desperately needed team practices before going to Moscow. Guess how many people showed up at the Toronto airport to wish Team Canada good luck in Moscow?"

"I don't know," Andy said while shrugging his shoulders. "Five thousand, maybe?"

"Nobody."

"What? Nobody?" Andy was genuinely surprised.

"That's right. Not one single Canadian fan."

"Really? That must have made the guys on the team feel bad."

"Everyone likes a winner and no one likes a loser. After all the booing the team got in Vancouver and all the negative criticism in the press it was not surprising that no one showed up to wish them 'Bon voyage et bonne chance!' On the way to Sweden Sinden concluded that inviting 35 players to join the team was a mistake and that he should have picked a smaller team to work with. He decided that in Sweden he would concentrate on the players who were most likely to play in the games in Moscow, and they would essentially consist of the guys that won Game 2 in Toronto.

The visit to Stockholm provided the Canadians with an opportunity to adjust to the time zone difference and get over the jet lag. It would also allow them to get some experience with European officiating and get used to the larger international ice surface. Do you know what the difference is between the international and NHL rinks?"

"The international ones are bigger," Andy said knowingly.

"Yes, but how much bigger?"

"I'm not sure. I think they may be a bitter longer."

"Actually, they tend to be the same length but the international size rinks are wider by about a dozen feet. The larger surface was more suitable for the Soviet crisscross passing system because there was more open space. The Canadians weren't familiar with the larger ice surface so that was something they would have to get used to, and fast.

The two refs who officiated the two exhibition games in Sweden were the West Germans Franz Baader and Josef Kompalla. Tony Esposito was in nets for the first game. Unfortunately, it was not a pretty game. The Canadians coaches and players complained that the Swedes played rough and it was always from behind, never in front. Henderson wrote that the Swedes butt-ended and speared the Canadians every chance they got and interference seemed to be their sole game strategy. Throughout the game they were spearing, holding, interfering, and most of all, backstabbing."

"I think I know what interference is but what's backstabbing? I never heard that before," Andy asked.

"Interference is when a player who does not have the puck has his progress blocked by an opposing player. Basically, it's getting in the way of someone who does not have the puck. Doing that should result in a penalty. Backstabbing is a term that was used in the NHL for a check delivered directly from behind that shoves a player's face into the boards. Players wouldn't do that in the NHL unless they were looking for a fight. When the Swedes did it to Team Canada players, the Canadians swung around and let the guy have it with a cross-check. The Canadians ended up getting the majority of the penalties. Phil Esposito wrote that the Swedes were dirty players who used their sticks to spear the Canadians. He then added 'to tell the truth, we played as dirty as they did and maybe dirtier. But they started it by spearing, and even though it was an exhibition game, boy, we went after them with both barrels. Beating them up was more important to us than winning.' I did not see the games in Sweden on television, but when I read about the violence in them, I suspected that the Canadians were probably in a foul mood after the game in Vancouver and were taking their frustration out on the Swedes.

Sinden tried to raise his concerns about the Swedes getting away with infractions with the referees during the first two periods but they were oblivious to the issues and acted as though they had no idea what he was talking about. Sinden got the impression that they thought the Canadians were just a bunch of crybabies who complained because they were not playing particularly well in the game."

"Not playing well? What was the final score in the first game?"

"Canada won 4-1."

"Sounds to me like they played well!" Andy said approvingly.

"Things got worse in the second game. Ed Johnston got his first opportunity to play in nets for Team Canada. There was a particularly ugly incident towards the end of the first period.

However, there are different accounts of what happened and it is still somewhat of a mystery to me. One version that is recounted in some books is that Wayne Cashman was charging after Swedish player Ulf Sterner and continued to do so after the referee had blown his whistle. The standard narrative is that Sterner jabbed his stick into Wayne Cashman's mouth and tore his tongue open along its length.

Phil Esposito wrote that the Swede hit Cashman in the mouth with his stick and Cashman's tongue was slit wide open so that he looked like a snake. However, Ferguson's account was that the Swede speared Cashman in the mouth and nearly split his tongue. Henderson wrote that Cashman nearly had his tongue ripped out. Several accounts indicate that Cashman went to the dressing room and then to a hospital and that his tongue was stitched up. However, the number of stitches used to sew Cashman's tongue together again varies from book to book. In another version of the story, the Swede's stick did not penetrate Cashman's mouth at all. Instead, Cashman ran into the boards and bit his tongue causing his own injury all by himself and it was doubtful that Cashman got any stitches on his tongue. After reading these different accounts I can't say with certainty what exactly happened except that Cashman was hurt in the mouth and he did not play in the rest of the series. If that was not enough to spoil things, there was another big incident in the second game."

"What happened this time?"

"When there were about five minutes left in the game Hadfield was run into the boards from behind by Lars-Erik Sjoberg and retaliated with a high stick. Hadfield ended up breaking Sjoberg's nose."

"Oh, oh! What happened then?"

"The Swedish player collapsed on the ice. Apparently, he waved off the trainer who came to help him and skated around displaying his bleeding nose so journalists could take pictures that were in the newspapers the next day. Hadfield got a five-minute major penalty. While these regrettable incidents spoiled the game, they had an unintended beneficial consequence."

"Like what, Gramps?"

"Ferguson wrote that such incidents helped bring the team together."

"Did it bring the team together enough to win the game?"

"No! But they didn't lose either. Just before the end of the game, the Swedes were winning 3-4 and fortunately, Phil Esposito scored a short-handed goal to tie it up 4-4."

"Good! Way to go, Esposito!" Andy said, relieved that Team Canada had not lost.

"Although the two exhibition games with the Swedes were not pretty, at least they were over. However, the experience fueled Sinden's continuing worry about the inferiority of the international two-referees system which was compounded by what he considered to be the ineptitude of the two West German referees who were also scheduled to officiate some of the upcoming games in Moscow. Sinden believed that because there were only two officials instead of three on the ice, the Swedes were able to get away with unsportsmanlike conduct behind the officials' backs. Sinden also noted that the Soviets had already demonstrated in the games in Canada that they were masters in the technique of interference and he did not like the thought of the refs letting the Soviets get away with it in Moscow."

"Masters in interference? How did they do it?" Andy asked.

"Sinden described how if one of the Soviets was late coming back up ice, he'd make sure that the last Canadian player coming up ice on the attack wouldn't get back into the play. The Soviet player would interfere and get in the way but they got away with it because it all happened behind the referee's back."

"Were there any other things they would do?"

"Sinden said that the Soviets also got away with interference in the offensive zone even when right in front of the referees. For example, when the Soviets were on a power play one of their players would get near the Canadian net and set up a block on one of the Canadian defencemen. Then one of the Soviet open players would break for the net to take a pass without any defenceman getting in his way. Regardless of whether or not the referees would penalize the Soviets when they engaged in interference, the general opinion among the Canadian coaches and players was that Baader and Kompalla, who were supposed to be two of the best referees in Europe, were lousy referees. Sinden thought they were unfair and poor skaters who were far behind the play throughout the games. On top of it all, he didn't think the refs had a firm grasp of the rules."

"What made him think that?" Andy asked.

"Sinden described a situation in the second period of the second game in Stockholm when Phil Esposito was penalized for cross-checking. However, one of the referees assessed him a misconduct penalty. You couldn't assess a misconduct for cross-checking. The referee was confused with spearing for which he could assess a misconduct. Sinden thought the two referees were incompetent and contributed to spoiling the games. Sinden had no idea how good or bad the Swedish and Czechoslovak referees who were scheduled to officiate some games in Moscow were, but he believed the West Germans had something against Team Canada and he hoped to see as little of them as possible. If the quality of the officiating was not enough of a problem for the coaches and team, they got some more discouraging news before leaving Sweden."

"What discouraging news?" Andy asked.

"It sounded as if a large segment of the Canadian population had quit on them. Many sports commentators criticized Team Canada's performance in Canada and Sweden and the media frequently referred to Canadian players as bullies, gangsters, and animals. An increasing portion of the media and the Canadian public now expected the Canadians to lose in Moscow and blow the series. That negative media commentary compounded the unpleasant experiences of being booed in Vancouver and the hostility the team encountered on the ice in Sweden. However, sometimes there's a silver lining to negative developments. Remember what I said about there often being fortune in misfortune?"

"How could there be anything good from all the criticism?"

"Try to imagine that you were a member of Team Canada. Although the players were not surprised to see that they were lambasted in the Swedish press, reading the condemnation in the Canadian press was tough to take. The players came to feel as though it was just them against everyone else. More than ever they realized that they were going to have to pull together if they were going to succeed. One of the benefits of going to Sweden was that the players could not go home after practices. As a result, they and their spouses spent time together and got to know each other. The players who were adversaries on different teams during the NHL season had become friends. The Swedish interlude became a critical turning point in the team's growth and transformation. It brought the members of Team Canada closer together as a team and turned out to be a blessing in disguise. The adversity from every side helped the team to gel and it manifested itself on the ice. The team practice after the second game in Sweden was the best one since the team was created and the players felt their conditioning was improving.

On 20 September Team Canada flew from Sweden to Moscow. Everyone saw them as the underdogs going to Moscow. When they left Sweden, the Canadian players thought they were on their own. They felt that they were going to fight for themselves in the remaining games and no one else since they didn't seem to have the support they expected from home.

But the situation was a little more complex than that. Although the critics were making a lot of noise at the time and made it seem that a lot of the Canadian public had turned their backs on Team Canada, there were tons of Canadians, like me, who supported our team from day one. Win or lose, our loyalty was to our team and country. So while Team Canada was playing and practicing in Sweden, what do you think the Soviets did during the break before the games in Moscow?"

"I bet they kept practicing every day," Andy answered.

"Nope! Some of the Soviet players returned to their club teams to play in some games. However, all the others took a break from hockey and rested. The Soviet team did not resume practicing until three days before the first game in Moscow."

"Why did they take the break?"

"I guess they were now the ones now who were overconfident and sure they would win the series."

By this time Andy and his grandfather had been canoeing for a while and had made a circle around the lake. They were approaching their cottage when Floyd said "Let's go back to the cottage and take our own break for lunch. I'll tell you about the rest of the series and what happened in Moscow afterward."

CHAPTER 8:
GAME 5 IN MOSCOW

After all the paddling on the lake, Andy enjoyed lunch with his grandparents. The pitcher of lemonade on the dining table was half full when they had finished eating. Floyd said, "C'mon Andy. Let's take the lemonade outside and I'll tell you what happened in Moscow." They both settled comfortably into wooden Adirondack chairs and looked out over the lake in front of them. Floyd picked up the story where he had left off.

"When Team Canada arrived in Moscow, they settled into the twenty story Intourist hotel which was reserved for foreigners. Not only did Team Canada show up with its entourage, so did 3,000 Canadian hockey fans who went all the way to Moscow to cheer the team on. When the series was announced a limited number of package deals were made available to the Canadian public that included airfare, hotel, and tickets to the four games. They were gobbled up in no time. The Canadian fans who traveled to Moscow stayed at the same Intourist hotel."

"You didn't mention before if any Soviet tourists came to Canada to cheer on their team. Were there any?" Andy asked.

"None. When the Soviets came to Canada, they did not bring any wives, girlfriends, parents, other family members, friends, or fans. The Soviet authorities claimed to follow a policy of 'no distractions'. However, in those days it was very difficult for average Soviet citizens to get a passport and permission to travel abroad and any time a Soviet would obtain special permission to travel abroad, the other family members would typically have to stay behind so the person who went abroad would be more likely to return and not stay in the West. One has to admit that the lack of any Soviet fans in the stands during the games in Canada to cheer on their team made the Soviet victories even more impressive."

"The Canadian fans in Moscow must have made the Canadian players happy, eh?"

"They sure did. However, there were some problems with the accommodations for everyone. Unfortunately, the hotel that the Canadians stayed at was far from first-class and some accounts compared the rooms to those of a student residence in college. The poor quality of available food was also a common complaint. Team Canada anticipated this problem and before going to Moscow they arranged to import 300 frozen steaks with them for their pre-game meals, as well as some other things like beer and soft drinks. They knew that getting stuff like that in Moscow would be a problem.

The four games in the Soviet Union were all played in Moscow at the Luzhniki Ice Palace. When the team checked out the rink where the games would be held, they were surprised by some of the things that were different from the rinks in the NHL. Besides being of international dimensions and wider, the corners were squarer. Also, instead of having Plexiglas above the boards at both ends of the rink, there was wire-mesh netting. The netting provided some degree of rebound when a puck was shot at it. The Canadians were not familiar with that feature. With no glass on the sides of the rink, the Canadians had to make changes to how they moved the puck up and out of their zone.

Remember that at the end of the trip to Sweden, I said that the team came together?"

"Yeah..."

"Well, three guys, Vic Hadfield, Richard Martin, and Jocelyn Guevremont who went to Moscow with the team decided to quit before the first game in Moscow. They were disappointed that they were not playing, or not playing as much as they would have liked. They informed Sinden that they wanted to go back and join their respective NHL team's training camp to get ready for the upcoming season. To many observers, it looked as though they thought Team Canada was going to lose the series and they did not want to stick around a losing cause. The coaching staff did not try to dissuade the three because they wanted to get rid of any negative vibes that might spoil the morale of the rest of the players. Arrangements were made for them to take the next available flight back home."

"The three of them leaving must have made the rest of the team feel bad, I guess," Andy suggested.

"Actually, it made the rest of the team more determined than before. Game 5 took place on Friday, September 22. All the games from Moscow were broadcast live using satellite technology which was not as sophisticated then as it is now. Because of the time difference, the Moscow games were shown on Canadian television much earlier in the day. My teacher, Mr. Cousineau, brought a television on a wheeled stand into the classroom. The same thing happened in classrooms across Canada. We all understood that the games in this series were historic events. But I already knew that."

"Who were the refs?" Andy asked.

"Uwe Dahlberg and Rudy Bata. Who do you think the coach picked to be the goalie?"

"Tony Esposito?" Andy guessed.

"That's right. Tony had a win and a tie in Canada while Dryden had two losses. Tony also played in the 4-1 win in the first game in Sweden while Dryden had not played since the game in Vancouver. Regarding the rest of the players, Sinden had already decided to use a smaller group of core players, mostly composed of those who won Game 2 in Toronto. Thus, some players would not get a chance to play. On the forward line, Bill Goldsworthy and Dennis Hull were scratched. Jean Ratelle, Pete Mahovlich, and J.-P. Parisé were inserted. On defence, Don Awrey was replaced by Guy Lapointe. Despite being down in the series, the Canadians headed into Game 5 with confidence. They had no illusions about the Soviet team and respected their opponents enough now to know that any overconfidence was misguided.

The Canadians also had a much better idea of what to expect from the Soviet team. They knew how the Soviets cycled the puck. If a play did not evolve satisfactorily, the Soviets would cycle back and start over. They realized that the Soviets used set plays and would eventually hit the Canadian blue line coming down a lane. The Canadians made corresponding adjustments in their playing to be there at the right time. No matter how often the Soviets made their crisscross passes, by the time they got to the blue line a Canadian would be there to check them. The Soviets were not used to being checked into the boards as hard and as often as they were subjected to by the Canadians. Another adjustment the defencemen made because of the larger ice surface was being careful not to go into the corners during a penalty kill situation because the defencemen would not be able to get back in front of the net quickly afterward if the Soviet player in the corner quickly passed it to a teammate. So guess how big the Luzhniki Ice Palace was."

"I don't know. Pretty big," Andy pondered.

"The arena's seating capacity was a little smaller than a typical NHL arena and accommodated about 13,500 fans. The 3,000 Canadians in the stands made a loud and boisterous group. The Soviet fans were subdued and relatively quiet. That was in part due to the presence in the arena of a large number of security personnel. The Soviets did not cheer and yell like the Canadians and generally expressed their displeasure during the games, especially when critical of something a Canadian player had done, by whistling. Remember how Prime Minister Trudeau attended the first game in Montreal?"

"Yeah..."

"Well, Leonid Brezhnev, the General Secretary of the Communist Party of the Soviet Union, was there, as well as President Nikolai Podgorny and Prime Minister Alexei Kosygin. Their presence demonstrated how important the series was to the Soviets too. The television broadcast started with the usual pre-game opening ceremonies. Something hilarious happened during the ceremony that made a lot of people laugh."

"What was that?"

"A group of young skaters came on the ice and presented each player with flowers. That was followed by player introductions. A piece of the stem from one of the flowers had fallen on the ice and when Phil Esposito was introduced, he took a stride forward and slipped on the flower stem."

"Did he fall down?"

"He sure did! Esposito fell on his butt with his legs in the air. Everyone laughed in the stands, including the Canadians. Although it was somewhat embarrassing Esposito managed to turn things around. He made a theatrical gesture of bowing to the crowd which got him a round of applause. He then clowned around by holding onto the boards when skating back."

"Ha! Ha!" Andy imagined what the episode must have looked like and laughed.

"That episode released a lot of pent-up tension in the air. Then the game got underway and in the first period both teams had a penalty that they killed off. Just after the fifteenth minute, Rod

Gilbert passed to Gilbert Perreault who took the puck in deep in the Soviet zone drawing the defencemen with him. He then passed to Parisé in the slot who shot the puck through the five hole and scored. Canada was up 1-0."

"All right! Canada scored first!"

"Everyone in my class cheered. That first goal caused everyone to perk up. When the period finished, Mr. Cousineau turned down the volume on the television and tried to give us a lesson during the intermission but we were so distracted by the game that we did not really pay attention to him and just waited for the next period to start. The reception on the television was not the best and there were frequent blackouts on the screen, but we didn't care. Unlike the NHL games from distant cities, the fuzzy television images made it clear that the game was being played far, far, away, and on the other side of the planet. Then the second period started with a bang."

"What happened?"

"At the two-and-a-half-minute mark of the second period, Bobby Clarke won a faceoff in the Soviet zone and the puck went to Henderson who passed it back to Clarke who drove to the net and fired a backhander in the five hole. Canada was up 2-0. Once again, we all cheered in class. The game was starting on the right track and it continued. At the twelfth-minute mark, Guy Lapointe fired a slapshot towards the Soviet net which was blocked by a Soviet player. However, Henderson picked up the rebound and shot the puck into the right corner of the net. The game was just a little over the halfway point and even though Team Canada had taken a couple of penalties, it was leading 3-0."

"That's a great lead!" Andy said.

"I couldn't imagine anything being more fun than the experience of cheering with my classmates as Team Canada established such a commanding lead. But we had to hold on to our horses! This series was full of surprises and there were more speed bumps on the road than you could imagine. At that point in the game, we all got a huge scare and a reminder that wearing a helmet like the Soviet players did was a good idea."

"Why? What happened?" Andy asked anxiously.

"On Henderson's next shift after scoring the third goal he was racing for the puck at full speed and just after crossing the Soviet blue line was about to fire a shot at the net when a Soviet player who was chasing him tripped him from behind. Henderson fell to the ice and slammed into the end boards. He hit his head so hard that he was knocked out cold. Henderson was unconscious and just lay there on the ice. The Canadian players rushed toward him along with the team trainer who tried to revive him. Henderson eventually came around and regained consciousness. He was then slowly escorted back to the dressing room. A doctor told him he had suffered a concussion and should not play in the game anymore. Henderson had some experience with concussions. He did not initially play in the NHL with a helmet but after a couple of concussions in junior hockey and the NHL he started wearing a helmet in 1966. Thank God Henderson was wearing one in this game or his injury would have been much worse! Henderson wrote that if he had not worn that helmet he might have been killed."

"Did Henderson stop playing in the game?" Andy asked.

"Are you kidding? No way! Henderson begged the coach to let him play. Sinden told him he could play if he wanted to. The impact of a concussion was not as well understood then as it is today. There's no way today that Henderson would be allowed to play so quickly after such an injury. But Henderson went back to the bench and probably had a splitting headache! No matter what the circumstances, Henderson was determined. He had an incredible fighting spirit. So Team Canada had a 3-0 lead at the end of the second period. Looking good, right?"

"I'd rather be up by three than down by three," Andy said.

"Me too. Then at the three-and-a-half-minute mark of the third period, Vladimir Petrov stole the puck from a Canadian defenceman at the blue line and passed it to Yuri Blinov who had a breakaway and scored. The Soviets got their first goal and it was 3-1."

"Aww..."

"And then Henderson came to the rescue. Just before the fifth minute of the third period Clarke fired a long pass between two Soviet defencemen that Henderson rushed to pick up. He then zeroed in on Tretiak and scored. Can you believe that? He had just suffered a concussion and scored his second goal of the game! Canada's three-goal margin was now re-established at 4-1 and there were only fifteen minutes left in the game. My class cheered like crazy and I was feeling ecstatic! The Canadian fans in the Moscow arena cheered and made a lot more noise than the Soviets in the stands. Around that time, they started chanting 'Nyet, Nyet, Soviet! Da, Da, Kanada!'"

"What does that mean?" Andy asked.

"'No, No, Soviet! Yes, Yes, Canada!' But just when some people thought we had the game in the bag, the game's momentum took a dramatic shift. According to Sinden, after a slow start in the first period, the Canadians took control of the game and had the Soviets on the run at the end of the second period. However, beginning in the third period, the bottom fell out and the Canadian players stopped skating and he had no idea why. Henderson wrote that the team had reverted to typical NHL thinking. They had a commanding lead and thought they could coast to the end of the game. In the process, they lost their concentration, which was suicide when playing against the Soviets who would pounce on turnovers and get their transition game going before you could blink. You're not going to believe what happened next."

"What? What happened?" Andy asked anxiously.

"Starting in the ninth minute, Anisin, Shadrin, Gusev, and Vikulov scored four consecutive Soviet goals in less than six minutes. The goals by Anisin and Shadrin were just eight seconds apart. The mood in my classroom steadily plummeted as we watched Canada's lead evaporate. At one point when the score was tied 4-4 a Canadian player hit the post. Everything could have changed if the puck had deflected into the net. I prayed that the Canadians would score a game-winning goal but instead the Soviets scored on a breakaway."

"Oh, no!"

"Yeah, it was a disaster. The game ended with Team Canada losing 4-5. Everyone in the class was shocked and speechless. It was terrible. The Canadians had played so well and had a three-goal lead but then they let up for a few minutes and that it was all it took for the Soviets to score a bunch. However, as the Team Canada players skated off the ice the 3,000 Canadian fans in the arena gave them a standing ovation and showed they were 100% behind Team Canada. Their support helped boost the team's morale but not everyone in my class was confident. I remember talking with my classmates after the game. All the discussions revealed those who were true die-hard Canadian hockey fans like me and those who were pessimists about the likely outcome. I refused to give in to their pessimism. I simply could not imagine that my hockey heroes like Yvan Cournoyer would lose and that the Soviets were 'better'.

Yet, the situation was bleak. After five games the Soviets had won three, the Canadians one, and there was one tie. There were three games left in the series. The Soviets now seemed to have a stranglehold on the series. If they won just one more game, they would win the series. The only way that Team Canada could win the series was by winning each of the three remaining games. In theory, it was possible. However, it would require the Canadian players to play the best hockey they ever played in their lives.

After school, I walked home and reflected on all the things that contributed to this miserable scenario and wondered why they had to play the series in September when they were out of condition? Why didn't they start preparing earlier? Why didn't they have enough time to develop the team chemistry? Why didn't they know more about what the Soviet team and figure out before the series began what they would have to do to neutralize them? Why did Bobby Orr have to have his knee problems now? And where was Bobby Hull when you needed him? The period right after Game 5 was the most depressing point in the series. It felt like rock bottom. The suspense and tension were excruciating. Everything else was put on hold until this series with the Soviets was finally decided one way or another and the question of who was best was resolved once and for all."

"How did the coaches feel after the game? What did they say to the players?"

"After the game, Sinden went straight to the coaches' room and threw a coffee cup against the wall in frustration. He stayed in the room and neither he, nor Ferguson, went to the press conference. Sinden did not want to see any players either because he thought he would have said the wrong thing. He had said all he could throughout the previous six weeks. The players had heard more than enough from him. It was now up to the players to come up with their own answers.

Regarding the officiating, Sinden wrote that the referees, Dahlberg and Bata, did a good job by international standards but not by NHL standards. However, he indicated he would rather have those two referees than the West Germans who were scheduled to officiate the next game but that was impossible to change at that point. Ferguson had a more critical take on the officiating in Game 5. He wrote that the European officials were inferior to NHL officials and that they stank. He thought they were inconsistent and biased, illustrating the point with an example where a Soviet player high sticked Dennis Hull and nothing happened but when Phil Esposito high sticked a Soviet player Esposito got a penalty."

"What about the players, Gramps? How did they feel after the game?"

"It was a slightly different situation in the players' dressing room. After the game, the players were calm and confident. No one was freaking out or throwing tantrums. By then the coaches had pared the roster down and the team lineup was pretty well set for the remainder of the series. They did not expect a lot of changes in the final games. The team had come together and their conditioning was kicking in. Even though Team Canada was in a terrible situation, there was something the Canadian players had that was a big advantage in their favour."

"What was that?"

"All of the Canadian players had experience with long NHL seasons followed by the Stanley Cup playoffs. The players knew what it was like to play in series after series, often up to seven games, many determined only at the end, and some only in overtime. They knew what it took for a team to win a Stanley Cup. They had experience with losing tough games and bouncing back the next day. Being behind in a series and coming back was something they were familiar with. The Canadians knew what they had to do to win the series. No matter how exhausted and drained, they would have to come up with what it took to win. The players knew they could do it and could win the next three games. And they were determined to do it and fight to the last second."

"I wonder how the Soviets felt after the game? They must have been feeling great," Andy thought.

"The Soviets thought they had the series in the bag. They only needed to win one more game in the next three to win the series and they were sure that would happen. They were now experiencing some of that overconfidence the Canadians had displayed before the series began. And then Team Canada's coach had another problem to deal with."

"Really? What was that?"

"After the Game 5 loss, Gilbert Perreault decided to jump ship and go home. He said that he was not in shape and needed to get back to join his NHL team in Buffalo at their training camp. He was the fourth and last player to leave the team. Several members of the squad did not get to play much, if at all, including Bobby Orr, Marcel Dionne, Dale Tallon, Ed Johnston, Brian Glennie, and Mickey Redmond, but they stuck around and offered their support to the team rather than return home. Their support was appreciated by the rest of the team."

"Good for them!"

"And just when things looked bad after the loss in Game 5 and this fourth departure, there was a surprising development that contributed to injecting some positive energy and enthusiasm into the Team Canada dressing room."

"What was that, Gramps?"

"Team Canada discovered they were not alone and that thousands and thousands of Canadians were wishing them good luck. Besides the 3,000 cheering Canadian fans in the arena for each game, the team began to receive a ton of encouraging messages by telegram and telex as well as postcards from home. The team posted the messages along the wall in the corridor leading to their dressing room. After the games in Sweden, it seemed as if many Canadians no longer supported Team Canada and the players felt they were on their own. However, the tide had turned. Canadian fans who supported the team now expressed their support and the flood of positive messages from Canada made the players realize that they had the backing of the country after all. The series was doing something incredible for Canadian national unity! More and more people wanted Team Canada to succeed!

No one could tell the future and what the outcome would be but one thing we could tell for sure: the players on Team Canada were going to play their best. In the process, they would put on a show unlike anything the hockey world had seen before. Those of us who saw it will never forget it."

CHAPTER 9:
GAME 6 IN MOSCOW

"Game 6 was played on Sunday, 24 September. In the period leading up to the game, I felt so much pressure and stress that I worried myself sick! Team Canada was going into Game 6 with only one win in the previous five games, and that was on September 4 which was almost three weeks earlier and seemed like ages ago. I watched the game on the television at home with my father.

The referees were the two that has officiated the games in Stockholm, Franz Baader and Josef Kompalla. Sinden decided to give Dryden his third chance at goaltending in this series. Dryden had let in 12 goals in two games but the coach had faith in him. Besides, Sinden had already decided that the workload and pressure were too much for just one goalie and continued to believe that he needed to rotate the goalies to win the series. Sinden decided that in the last three games, Dryden would play Games 6 and 8 and Tony Esposito would play in Game 7.

Having observed the characteristics of the Soviet team and how it played hockey in the first five games, Dryden decided that he would have to change his goaltending style. The games that he was used to in the NHL were end-to-end type of games where the forwards would head for the net and take a shot. NHL goalies would come out of the net to cut the angles and provide less of a net to shoot at. However, the Soviet style of playing hockey was more of a side-to-side crisscrossing game. It was more of a passing game than a shooting one. If the goalie moved away from the goal line in anticipation of a shot, a Soviet player who received a pass on the side of the goal would have an open net. Also, by moving out of the goal, a pass to a Soviet player on the side would require the goalie to make a wider lateral movement. Accordingly, Dryden decided to change his goaltending style and stay closer to the goal line. In the middle of the series, Dryden did not have much time to practice the new tactic and overcome his previously-acquired and ingrained instincts. This was an example of how one Canadian player assessed the situation and made corresponding adjustments to his playing style.

An example of Team Canada adjusting its style was described by Ferguson. Winning the remaining games would require finding a flaw in the Soviet armament. The coaches believed the Soviets' relatively poor defensive work in their zone was a flaw that they needed to exploit. Sinden and Fergusen concluded that the Canadian players needed to pressure the Soviet defencemen more than in previous games. The coaches devised new drills for their practices to adjust their game to exploit perceived Soviet weaknesses. In one drill they had five attackers working against three defenders while passing the puck as frequently as possible and maintaining possession of it for as long as possible.

For Game 6 the coaches took winger Frank Mahovlich and defenceman Rod Seiling out of the lineup. Centre Red Berenson and winger Dennis Hull were added to the forward line. Serge Savard's ankle had sufficiently healed that he was added to the defence. The three defensive pairings for the game were Savard and Lapointe, Park and Bergman, and Stapleton and White. Those guys had a lot riding on their shoulders. They simply could not allow the Soviets to score five goals as in the previous game. However, by this stage in the series, the Canadians also discovered another advantage that they had."

"What was that, Gramps?"

"By this time, the Soviets were overconfident and believed that their victory in the series was inevitable. They were so confident that they were going to win that according to some accounts the coaches allowed the players to go home between games. Because the Soviets had so much success in the first five games, they didn't consider making any significant changes to their playing style to be necessary. The Soviets decided to stick with only one goalie despite the cumulative pressure that consecutive games put on Tretiak and only made a few roster changes."

"I don't get it. How was any of that an advantage to the Canadians?"

"By then the Canadians had detected the subtleties in the way the Soviets played the game. The Soviets had set plays and patterns for breaking out of their zone, crisscrossing on rushes, passing instead of shooting, and other things. The Soviets consistently used the set plays with set units and the Soviet coaches expected the players to stick to the choreographed plays rather than resort to individual creativity and improvisation on the ice. Of course, this is a generalization and there are always exceptions and surprises in game situations but set plays were a predominant characteristic of the Soviet style of playing hockey. By this stage in the series, the Canadians found the Soviets to be predictable and could anticipate what they were likely to do next throughout the game. Being able to correctly predict what your opponent is going to do is a huge advantage because you can then sabotage their plans and break up their plays."

"Okay, I get it," said Andy.

"Before Game 6 Sinden told the players not to think about the past or future games. They had to focus on the game they were playing and take it one period at a time. That was the Canadian game plan. The players were to concentrate on their next shift and avoid making any errors. Are you ready for Game 6, Andy?"

"Sure am, Gramps!"

"Okay! In the first period, Bergman got a tripping penalty and then Phil Esposito got a double minor for charging. Fortunately, the Soviets did not score during their extended power play. The first period ended with no goals. However, the second period started badly. Just after the first minute, Yuri Lyapkin fired a slapshot at the Canadian net while Dryden was screened and scored the first Soviet goal of the game. So Canada was down 0-1."

"Oh, crap!" Andy mumbled.

"I was so unhappy when they scored but I had seen so many Soviet goals by then that I did not react. Neither did my father. Then four minutes later the Canadians put on the pressure and Rod Gilbert fired a couple of shots towards the Soviet goal. One hit a defenceman and Gilbert managed to recover the rebound and took another shot at the net. Tretiak fell to the ice while Dennis Hull recovered a rebound and shot it over Tretiak into the net. The score was now tied 1-1."

"That's better!"

"A minute later the Canadians again put the pressure on and when Red Berenson got the puck behind the Soviet net he passed it toward the centre and Cournoyer slapped it in the net. It only took a minute for Canadians to take a 2-1 lead."

"All right Canada! That's the way to do it!" Andy said with a smile.

"Just fifteen seconds after the second Canadian goal one of the Soviets tried to pass the puck out of their zone towards the centre but Henderson intercepted the pass, crossed the blue line, split the defencemen, and fired a snapshot before Tretiak could blink. Boom!

Canada was up 3-1. Team Canada scored three goals in one minute and twenty-three seconds. Pretty good, eh?"

"Holy smokes! That was like the Soviets' four goals in six minutes during the last game!" Andy said.

"Exactly. This series was full of surprises. What followed was a string of penalties. Lapointe and a Soviet were both sent to the box for roughing. The referees also blew the whistle on the Canadians for a couple of offsides that could have led to scoring chances. In two cases the replays showed that the Canadians were onside. The officiating was an issue from the beginning of the game. The Canadians thought the referees were awful and not up to the standards required of a game of this calibre and importance.

Then just after the ten-minute mark in the second period something happened that was a significant event in the series that I did not notice and register at the time but only found out about much later. Kharlamov was always a problem for the Canadians. He was fast and could fire a puck with pinpoint accuracy. At one point in the game while Ferguson was standing behind Team Canada's bench he said that somebody had to get Kharlamov. Bobby Clarke understood that what Ferguson had said constituted instructions to hit Kharlamov. A little later in the game, Kharlamov had the puck and Clarke chased after him. Just after Kharlamov made a pass Clarke swung his stick and slashed Kharlamov in the ankle pretty hard."

"Ouch! That wasn't very nice."

"No, it wasn't. I wished he hadn't done that. Clarke got a penalty for slashing and a ten-minute misconduct. He would subsequently be quoted as having said that he would have never gotten out of Flin Flon if he had never learned to lay a two-hander."

"What does that mean?"

"Flin Flon is the town in Manitoba where Clarke was born and played junior hockey with the Flin Flon Bombers. The 'two-hander' term that he used describes swinging a hockey stick like an axe with two hands. In the NHL if the referees saw something like that, they would penalize the perpetrator. However, whether or not the perpetrator was penalized, every team had a goon or two who were known as 'enforcers' who would try to teach the guy who did it a lesson. Ferguson was considered one of those enforcers when he played for the Canadiens."

"So what happened to Kharlamov?" Andy asked.

"Kharlamov did not fall to the ice when he was slashed and he continued to play in the game. However, he did not play in the next game and only returned in game 8. Some books suggest that his ankle was fractured. A lot of people thought Kharlamov was the best Soviet player and that slashing him had a big impact on the series but others were not convinced."

"Why not?"

"Well, hockey is a team sport and the Soviets had a roster of very talented players who could take his place. Kharlamov had the most penalty minutes on the Soviet team and wasn't their team's leading scorer. Ellis had done a fantastic job shadowing Kharlamov and he only scored three goals in the seven games that he played in."

"How many assists did he get?" Andy asked.

"Four."

"That's seven points in seven games. That's pretty good!"

"True. But there was another Soviet player who also had seven points and two others who had even more. But there's something else that always comes to mind when I think about that slash on Kharlamov. When I first found out about that slash, I felt pretty bad. I still do. However, the incident would have stood out more if the Soviets' behaviour was beyond reproach. Fighting is not tolerated in international hockey and players who fight get ejected from the games. So the Soviets used their sticks to spear which was less common in the NHL and the Canadian players complained about the Soviets' swordsmanship. Phil Esposito said the Soviets did things to the Canadians that he had never experienced before. Clarke said that the Soviets did a lot of dirty things like kicking out the legs of Canadian players from behind. I had never seen any NHL player attempt to injure another player with the blade of his skate but in this series, there was a particularly ugly incident when a Soviet player did that to a Canadian player and drew blood. We'll get to that later. There were a lot of dirty things and cheap shots done on the ice by both sides during the series. None of that is an excuse for the slash on Kharlamov but that was the context."

"Okay, Gramps! You left off in the second period and Canada was up 3-1. What happened after the slash?"

"Right. Well, with less than three minutes left in the second period, Dennis Hull got a penalty. Guess what it was for?"

"Slashing?"

"Right! And then guess what happened while the Soviets were on another power play?"

"They scored."

"Right again! Just nine seconds into the power play Yakushev scored and the score was 3-2. So Team Canada's lead was reduced to just one goal and it had to win this game so the situation was tense and explosive. One thing for sure, the game was not boring although it was not always pretty.

Thirty-five seconds later Phil Esposito got a five-minute penalty for high sticking and the Canadian bench freaked out. The coaches and players were convinced that the officiating was not only incompetent but biased in favour of the Soviets. The differences between North American and European officiating became clearer more than ever and Sinden and Ferguson were furious. In his book about the series, Sinden wrote that after two periods the Canadians had played 15 minutes shorthanded. In his opinion, the calls were malicious and he had a long-standing belief that there was only one way to stop a referee in a situation like that."

"What was that?"

"It was to ridicule the referees in front of the crowd, and in this case, the world, since the game was on TV throughout Europe and North America. Sinden and Ferguson wanted everyone to know that they thought the West German refs were incompetent and biased."

"So what did they do?"

"They made a scene. The Canadian bench threw towels on the ice and kept raging at the refs. Ferguson wrote that the West German referees were so bad that both he and Sinden yelled so much at them that they almost lost their voices! For all his yelling at the refs, Ferguson got a bench penalty. There were two minutes and 14 seconds left in the second period and Canada had to play two men short! Can you believe that? Canada was only leading by a goal and the Soviets had a tremendous advantage and opportunity to tie the game and possibly win it. Do you think my dad and I were sitting on the edge of our seats?"

"Well, yeah..."

"You bet we were. Remember how a Canadian goal was disallowed in Game 4?"

"Yeah, that was because the ref said it was kicked in?"

"Right! Well, there was a situation where the Soviets may have scored a goal but it did not count. At one point during their two-man advantage, the Soviets were passing the puck around in our zone and Yakushev passed it to Kharlamov at the side of the goal who one-timed at the net. The puck hit Dryden's pad and then deflected upwards towards the net and ended up in Dryden's glove. The Soviet players on the ice tried to convince the referee that the puck went in the net and bounced off the mesh and into Dryden's glove. Dryden was not sure if it hit the post or went inside the net. The goal judge and referees did not see it and did not think it went in. The referees ruled no goal. The video replay was inconclusive. The Soviets now felt like the Canadians had in Game 4 when a goal that could have changed the game's outcome was disallowed. Fortunately, the Canadians manage to fend off the Soviet power play and the second period ended with Canada maintaining their 3-2 lead."

"All right, Canada!"

"Remember after the game in Toronto how some Soviet officials were mad about the outcome of the game and blamed the referees for letting the Canadians get away with too many things that the Soviets thought should have been penalized and how they didn't have any problem going into the referees' dressing room to tell them off and kick a chair or two over?"

"Yeah..."

"The two referees in this game not only upset the Canadians on the bench but also Bobby Orr who was watching from the stands. Both Sinden and Orr wanted to have a word with the refs after they came off the ice during the second intermission. When the referees walked down the hall to their dressing room both Sinden and Orr chased after them. When the referees stopped Orr bumped into one of them. Within seconds the Soviet police and security officials surrounded them. They had to forget about challenging the refs and avoid being taken away by the police. Fortunately, Sinden and Orr managed to extricate themselves from that tense situation. When Sinden got to Team Canada's dressing room he knew he had to do something to get the players to calm down and recover their poise. They only had a one-goal lead and there were still 20 minutes left in the game. The Soviets had already demonstrated that they could score bundles of goals in short bursts. What do you think Sinden did?"

"Gave the team a pep talk?"

"He did that, but there was something else. He had someone check the status of the ice on the rink. It turned out that the Soviets had flooded the rink with too much water and Sinden wanted to wait for the water to adequately freeze. Some people assumed that the overflooding was deliberate and an attempt to slow the Canadians down on the ice. So while the Soviets and the referees were already on the ice and waiting to start the third period, Sinden kept the Canadian team in the dressing room for another five minutes. That turned out to have been a smart decision. The Canadians end up playing an outstanding period. They neutralized much of the Soviet play and did not get any penalties throughout the period until..."

"Until what?" Andy asked impatiently.

"Until the very end when there were just over two minutes left in the game. That's when the refs decided to call the only penalty of the period on Ron Ellis."

"For what?!" Andy asked.

"Holding! Ellis said that the call was ridiculous and to the guys on Team Canada it looked like the referees wanted to give the Soviets one last chance in the game. Sinden wrote that in the NHL referees didn't call penalties in the last two minutes unless there was a flagrant violation. He thought the penalty called on Ellis was not even close to flagrant."

"What happened? Did the Soviets score?"

"Fortunately, the Canadians managed to prevent that from happening. No goals were scored in the third and Canada won the game 3-2 with the game-winning goal coming from Paul Henderson."

"All right Team Canada! Way to go!" Andy said.

"My father and I had our butts glued to our seats and our eyes glued to the television screen throughout the whole game. We were so nervous throughout the third period as Canada protected its lead. Our relief only came with the end of the game and we were exhilarated by the victory. Team Canada emerged triumphant to fight another day. However, there was something really special about this win, besides the fact that it was a must-win game situation and that Team Canada pulled through."

"What's that, Gramps?"

"The penalties! Guess how many penalty minutes the Canadians got in this game compared to the Soviets?"

"Twenty to five or something like that?"

"It was worse than that! The Canadians had eight penalties for a total of 31 minutes. The Soviets only had two minors for a total of four minutes! Can you believe that? Even with so many more penalties than the Soviets, Team Canada managed to win the game."

"That's impressive!"

"It sure was, but the officiating was a real problem. Phil Esposito considered the referees to have done an awful job and was convinced they took instructions from the Soviets. The refs called penalties that never happened and the Canadians frequently played a man or two short, while the Soviets were on one power play after another. Sinden wrote that the referees were consistent and always bad. He considered the two refs in this game the most incompetent officials he had ever seen and believed that they did everything they could right up to the very end to help the Soviets. He was unhappy with their performance during the games in Sweden and now he was even more unhappy."

"I bet the Soviet coach was upset that his team had so many power plays and still lost."

"He must have been. After this game, Sinden and Fergusen went to the press conference but Soviet coach Bobrov did not show up. At the press conference, Sinden was asked about his behaviour towards the referees. He replied that Baader and Kompalla were so incompetent that he would meet with the Soviet officials the next day to ensure that they would not work in the series again. Remember how after the game in Toronto the Soviets asked for a change in the referees for the last two games in Canada?"

"Yes."

"And remember how they said that the hosts should be accommodating and in the spirit of friendship they should grant the Soviet wish and how the Canadians granted the Soviet request without any problems?"

"Yeah..."

"Well, now Sinden was going to find out whether the Soviets would reciprocate when the tables were turned. The next day the Canadian and Soviet officials had a meeting to determine which officials would work the eighth and final game. The Swede Uwe Dahlberg and the Czechoslovak Rudy Bata were scheduled to officiate Game 7 and Sinden made it clear that he did not want the West Germans Baader and Kompalla to officiate any more games. The Soviet authorities eventually agreed to Sinden's request and Dahlberg and Bata were scheduled to officiate both Games 7 and 8. Sinden thought the matter was settled. However, the Canadians had some other unexpected complications to deal with."

CHAPTER 10: UNEXPECTED COMPLICATIONS

"Unexpected complications? Like what?" Andy asked.

"Paul Henderson described how the Soviets engaged in all kinds of machinations, manipulating a variety of things to provide the Soviets with some sort of advantage and aggravate the Canadian players the whole time they were in Moscow. In his 1991 book Alan Eagleson emphasized that from the moment Team Canada arrived in Moscow they had daily problems with the Soviets to deal with. He described the problems as part of the psychological warfare that the Soviets waged on the Canadians.

Eagleson described two varieties of confrontations, those that happened on the ice and those that happened behind the scenes. He outlined a few of the behind-the-scenes variety. First, before they even got to Moscow, Team Canada was informed that there would be no hotel rooms for the wives of the players. Eagleson responded by saying that had the Soviet authorities better find rooms pronto or Team Canada would not travel to Moscow. Suddenly the rooms became available. However, when the players and their wives showed up, there were no double-size beds in the rooms but only twin beds that were perpendicular to one another rather than side by side in the centre of each room. When the players fixed the problem with some furniture shuffling the cost of the hotel room went up for the duration of the stay."

"What other problems did he have to deal with?" Andy asked.

"Here's another. When the Canadian players got to Moscow they visited the Luzhniki Ice Palace and found there were in fact two arenas, one big where the games would be played and another small one. The Soviets told Eagleson that the Canadians' dressing room was in the small arena. Eagleson had to argue with them to get a dressing room in the main arena but the newly-designated one was small, stank, and was about 150 yards away from the ice. On top of it all, it was full of junk. When the Canadians tried to clear it out, the police told them they were not allowed to move anything. So the Canadians went back at night and dumped everything in the hallway. If that was not enough of an inconvenience, it did not take long before they discovered that every night some of their equipment like sticks and skates would disappear even though the Canadians were supposed to have the only key to the lock on the door."

"Did they manage to stop their stuff from disappearing?"

"Yes. They had to mount a twenty-four hour guard. One of the training staff would stay there during the day and at night they got an employee from the Canadian embassy to sleep in the dressing room. That stopped the thefts of the equipment but there were other thefts to deal with."

"Like what?" Andy asked.

"Well, when Team Canada went to Moscow they imported some food, including steaks, beer, and soft drinks. It did not take long for some of the supplies to be stolen and disappear. You can imagine how the Canadian players felt when they learned that their steaks and beers were missing. And there were other unexpected problems."

"Now what?"

"There were a few tourist things to see in Moscow and Eagleson was advised that because the wives had paid tourist charter rates, they would get tickets to go see the Moscow Circus, the Bolshoi ballet, the Kremlin, and some other places. However, the Soviet hockey authorities indicated that they didn't have the money to pay for the tickets for the Canadian players to visit these sites. Eagleson had to negotiate with them and in the end, it cost the Canadians thousands of dollars which in those days was a heck of a lot of money. But tickets to tourist spots were not the only ticket problems that Eagleson had to contend with. He wrote that there was a need to get some game tickets for special guests who were late arrivals to Moscow. Tickets were available but the only way to get them was through individual officials with the Soviet Ice Hockey Federation."

"So what was the problem?" Andy wondered.

"The individuals supplying the tickets charged black market prices. It was as though the Soviets were scalping the tickets at inflated prices and lining their pockets. However, the players also had some other inconveniences to deal with."

"And what now?"

"According to Eagleson, whenever the Canadians arrived at the rink for their appointed practice times, the ice was always unavailable. There was either a fifteen-minute or twenty-minute wait or they were told that the rink was simply unavailable. On the morning after Game 5, the Canadian team showed up for their scheduled morning practice at the Luzhniki Arena only to find about a hundred kids skating around the rink. The arena officials told the Canadians to go somewhere else to practice. However, the Canadians solved that problem."

"How?" Andy asked.

"Eagleson got Dennis Hull and Rod Gilbert to get on the ice with a couple of pucks and start practicing their slapshots."

"What happened?"

"The rink emptied in no time. The team had their scheduled practice after all. At one practice while the team was on the ice in the late morning the Soviet coach Bobrov suddenly showed up and said that Team Canada had to vacate the ice so the Soviets could practice. Sinden showed Bobrov an itinerary that said the Canadians had the ice until half past noon and that the Soviets would get it afterward. Bobrov said the itinerary was wrong and he insisted that the Canadians had to get off the ice."

"What did Sinden do then?"

"Sinden told Bobrov that if he wanted to bring his players on the ice before 12:30 pm Sinden had no idea what might happen to them."

"Was there a fight?" Andy asked.

"No. Bobrov waited for his team's turn. But the Soviets had other ways of interfering and inconveniencing the Canadian players."

"What other ways?"

"Believe it or not, the Soviets tried to ruin the rest and sleep of the Canadian players by phoning them in their hotel rooms in the middle of the night. Whenever the players picked up the phones there would be silence on the other end of the line. In addition, the rooms in the hotel had an intercom system over which disturbing noises would be made in the middle of the night to prevent the Canadians from getting a good night's sleep. Phil Esposito wrote that one night after the phone rang and there was silence at the other end again, he was so fed up that he grabbed the phone cord and yanked it out of the wall but that did not solve the problem. A few minutes later there was a knock at the door and the hotel staff asked him to plug the phone back in. He couldn't because he had ripped the cord. So at four o'clock in the morning, the Soviets sent a repairman to fix it! The problem of the phantom phone calls disturbing the players' sleep did not occur just during the night. Henderson wrote that he tried to nap during the afternoon and would be similarly disturbed by the ringing phone with no one at the other end. He never had a good afternoon's sleep while in Moscow."

"That's crazy! I can't believe they would do such things."

"It just goes to show that this was not simply a series of friendly exhibition hockey games. It was war and according to Esposito and other players, the Soviets always had to have an edge, no matter what, and were always trying to pull something. The Canadians couldn't wait to get the games over with and leave the Soviet Union."

"It doesn't sound like the Soviets were very nice to Team Canada."

"Many of the ordinary Soviet citizens that the Canadians met were friendly but Soviet officials were a different story. However, the Canadians were also surprised by how the Soviet state sometimes treated its own citizens. Henderson wrote that the way people were treated in Russia was 'really unbelievable'. He gave an example that other players also described in their accounts. When kids in Moscow would watch the Canadian players practice, or would approach their bus, the Canadian players would sometimes throw some chewing gum or candies to the kids through the window. Western gum and candies weren't available in the Soviet Union and the kids were thrilled when the Canadian players would give them some. What do you think would happen then?"

"The kids would take the candy and eat it!"

"Not always. If a Red Army soldier was around he would take the candies and gum away. Soviet authorities evidently didn't want Soviet children to be exposed to Western sweets. Don't ask me what their problem was with Soviet kids tasting Western candy because I have no idea. Are you ready for what happened in Game 7?"

"Yes, sir!"

CHAPTER 11:
GAME 7 IN MOSCOW

"On Monday at school, my classmates and I chatted about the upcoming game and the series during every recess break and the lunch hour. The epidemic of hockey fever before Game 1 that had been contained for a few weeks now came back and people were feeling it from coast to coast. I had been suffering from the fever since Game 1.

Game 7 was held on Tuesday, 26 September. Mr. Cousineau brought a television into the classroom again so that we could watch the game during class time. I was grateful that he did that because I wanted to know what happened when it happened and would not have been able to concentrate on any classwork if I had had to wait until after school to find out the final score. As was the case with all the other games in the series, I felt that something historic was taking place. However, this game was even more special. If Canada lost, it would be curtains. Would Canada win or lose? Once again, I was pumped and the adrenaline was flowing. Everybody in the class was pumped. The whole country was pumped."

"Now I'm getting pumped, Gramps!"

"Using the same strategy in Game 6, Sinden told the Canadian players to focus on one period at a time and try to make each shift as productive as possible while avoiding making any mistakes. It was Tony Esposito's turn in nets. There were very few other changes in the lineup. Winger Bill Goldsworthy replaced Berenson and Sinden set up three centres and four wingers on each side."

"Did the Soviets make any changes?"

"The Soviets continued to believe that they would win either or both of the remaining two games and win the series so they didn't change their overall strategy. However, they made several changes to their lineup including designating seven defencemen to beef up their defence.

The referees for the game were Dahlberg and Bata, the same refs who officiated Game 5. Once the puck was dropped it did not take long for the action on the ice to heat up. In the fourth minute of the first period, Ellis emerged from a puck battle along the boards and passed it to Phil Esposito at centre who fired it in the five hole. Boom! Canada was up 1-0."

"Great start!" Andy exclaimed.

"Six minutes later there was a faceoff in the Soviet zone that the Soviets won. The puck was passed to Yakushev who passed the Canadian blue line and fired a slapshot that scored. So the game was tied 1-1. Penalties were called and at the sixteen-and-a-half-minute mark Vladimir Petrov scored while the Soviets were on a power play to give them a 1-2 lead."

"Aww..."

"We were all nervous but the Soviet lead did not last long. About a minute later there was a faceoff in the Soviet zone and the puck went back to Savard at the blue line. He passed it to Phil Esposito who took a quick wrist shot and sent it into the corner of the Soviet net to tie the game up 2-2 with just two and a half minutes left in the first period. Phil Esposito had scored both of Canada's goals. Boy, did my class cheer when Canada tied it up!

No goals were scored in the second period but there were plenty of penalties and the Canadians got most of them. Once again, the Canadians considered the refereeing to be one-sided and unfair.

The game was down to the final period, it was tied, and Canada had to win the game if they wanted to survive to Game 8. Just after the second-minute mark of the third period the action was in the Soviet zone and Rod Gilbert intercepted a Soviet pass behind the Soviet net and did a wrap-around to score on a backhand between Tretiak's pads."

"Woo hoo!"

"Woo hoo is right. Canada was up 3-2 and every time Canada scored my class erupted in cheers. As the game wore on the cheers for Team Canada became louder with each Canadian goal. The boos also got more intense with each Soviet goal like the next one. About a minute after Gilbert had scored Bergman got a penalty for holding and the Soviets were on a power play. Before the penalty expired Yakushev scored. So the game was tied at 3-3 and there were just under fifteen minutes left in the game. Canada had to score! Then something surprising happened that had not happened before in the series."

"What was that, Gramps?"

"As play went on the Soviets seemed to get a little frazzled and argue with each other on their bench. Normally, the Soviets kept their emotions under wraps but now it seemed that their frustration with the situation was coming to the surface as the Soviet players appeared to be blaming each other for their mistakes. Obviously, they wanted to settle the series with a victory in Game 7 so they wouldn't have to deal with the uncertainty of a final game to determine the outcome. It seemed like the pressure had finally gotten to them. So what do you expect to happen when the temperature rises and players are increasingly frustrated?"

"I don't know. Maybe some players make mistakes and someone scores a beautiful goal?" Andy pondered.

"Well, anything can happen, including mistakes and beautiful goals. In this case, with about three and a half minutes left in the game, the biggest fight of the series erupted and all hell broke loose."

"Oh, Oh! I bet the refs called some penalties!"

"They sure did. What happened was that Bergman held the puck against the boards behind the Canadian net and Boris Mikhailov ran into him and they started to tussle. The play was whistled dead but it seemed that Mikhailov had Bergman in a headlock and maintained his grip. Bergman went ballistic as he struggled to free himself. He tried to give Mikhailov a knuckle sandwich while the referees tried to get between them and separate the players. Mikhailov then did something that I have never seen before or since but only saw it when I watched the videotapes much later."

"What did he do?"

"He started to repeatedly kick Bergman with the blade of his skate. And guess what?"

"What?"

"Mikhailov's skate blade cut through Bergman's leg stocking, sliced his fiberglass shin pad, and Bergman's leg started bleeding. While Clarke's slashing Kharlamov's ankle in the previous game was certainly unsportsmanlike, I don't recall ever seeing a hockey player deliberately using the blade of his skates to slice an opposing player before. Ron Ellis later said that after the game he saw Bergman pour blood out of his skate. Anyway, when Cournoyer saw Mikhailov kicking Bergman he tried to land a few punches on Mikhailov and Yakushev then tried to neutralize Cournoyer. Esposito then got into the act and tried to stop Yakushev and everybody on the ice paired off and hung on to each other. When the melee was over the referees said they never saw Mikhailov do any kicking and they gave both Mikhailov and Bergman five-minute major penalties for roughing.

Once in the penalty box, Bergman pointed to Mikhailov and, in a not particularly subtle gesture, ran his finger across his throat. The series was an intense contest and this episode further confirmed it. Less than a minute and a half later something else dramatic happened."

"What?" Andy asked.

"Well, with just a little more than two minutes left in the game Paul Henderson put on a magic show just when Team Canada needed it most. The teams were playing four skaters a side and Team Canada had to do something to win the game. Paul Henderson had been sitting on the bench and thought that the coach might pull our goalie for an extra attacker, but that did not happen. Instead, he got on the ice for what was likely to be his final shift of the game. From the Canadian zone, Guy Lapointe passed the puck to Serge Savard who passed it up to Paul Henderson in the centre ice area. Henderson flew over the Soviet blue line and had two Soviet defencemen in front of him. The one on the left tried to swipe the puck with his stick as Henderson tried to put the puck through the defenceman's legs and the puck bounced off the inside of his skate. Henderson skated around the defender and picked up the puck again and headed towards the net. At that moment the other defender came across and tripped Henderson in an attempt to take him out."

"Did the ref blow the whistle for a penalty?"

"No. Something even better happened. Henderson fell to the ice, however, in an amazing display of athleticism, he managed to keep the puck on his stick and in front of him. At the same time, Tretiak dropped to his knees assuming that he could block the puck on the ice. The only way Henderson could score was to shoot it high."

"Is that what he did?"

"He sure did! Henderson wrote that he had just enough room to put a shot over Tretiak's shoulder and just under the crossbar. Boom! Like Foster Hewitt used to say 'He shoots! He scores!', only in this case, Henderson was sliding flat on the ice. Henderson later said that his winning goal in Game 7 was his best goal ever. You should have seen my class erupt when he scored. Everyone jumped up and down and the whole class cheered and hollered. We were so excited! Now imagine how many other Canadians across the country were doing that at the same time. Canada was now leading 4-3. But there was a problem."

"Now what?"

"The goal light did not come on. The goal judge did not signal that a goal was scored. Neither I nor my classmates were aware of the problem as we celebrated Henderson's goal. However, Team Canada's coaches noticed it. What would you do in such a situation if you were the coach?"

"I don't know. Start shouting at the referees and throw a couple of chairs on the ice?" Andy questioned with a chuckle.

"Close, but not quite. When the goal light did not come on Ferguson instantly feared that the Soviets would try to disallow the goal so he immediately ran up and down the bench and told the players to get on the ice and go over to congratulate Henderson and celebrate. Both he and Sinden literally pushed the players over the boards."

"Wow. What happened?"

"A few moments later the red light came on and the coaches called the players back to the bench. Nowadays you only see such bench-clearing celebrations when a team scores a winning goal in overtime."

"Did anything else happen during the last two minutes of the game?"

"Canada held on to the one-point lead and won the game 4-3. When it was over my class again erupted in cheers and we clapped in celebration. It is hard to describe how I felt. I was so proud of Team Canada. That team was representing our country and even though the situation looked terrible after Game 5, the two consecutive victories in Games 6 and 7 proved that Canada was not down and out but alive and kicking and still fighting to win. Everyone on the team was playing their best and doing incredible things. Henderson had suffered a concussion in Game 5 and went on to score a goal afterward. And now he had scored a second consecutive game-winning goal. Team Canada was proving itself to be a phenomenal team. How could you not be inspired by those guys? I was so excited it wasn't funny!

Both teams now had three wins and a tie. It would all boil down to the last game. Before the series started no one imagined that Team Canada would have to fight as hard as it did to come from behind just to tie the series and nobody thought it would all come down to the final game, winner takes all. Despite playing in the Soviet capital, Canada had the wind in its sails and some momentum. What's more, the team, and the country, had more confidence than before. No one was thinking about the previous losses. Everyone was now looking forward to Game 8.

Although the Soviets had been confident at the end of Games 4 and 5 that they were going to win the series, their failure to win in Games 6 and 7 dramatically changed the equation. Suddenly the inevitable victory was no longer a sure thing. The final game was shaping up to be the biggest one in Canadian and certainly one of the biggest in international hockey history. The final sixty minutes of hockey in the series would determine who could boast of being the best on the planet. The last game in the series was guaranteed to be dramatic as the stakes were the highest they had ever been and both teams were determined to win. However, even though the Soviets were playing at home, the Canadians had a distinct advantage."

"What was that?"

"The Soviets could never match the emotional intensity of the Canadian players on the ice. Nor could the Soviets match their desire to win. The Canadians wanted the victory more than the Soviets."

"I sometimes get emotional too during games but my coach always tells me to control myself!" Andy said somewhat confused by the mixed messages.

"Emotions can be a two-edged sword, Andy. Sometimes emotions can interfere with your judgment and make you do some silly things. It is often helpful to keep your emotions in check and think objectively about a problem. However, if something is important to you and if you care about it a lot, emotions can sometimes help you do some things that you might not have previously thought possible. The Canadian players reached deep down inside and came up with their secret weapon."

"What was that?"

"Their heart and soul. Putting your heart and soul into something it means you do it with all your energy and enthusiasm. With everything on the line, the Canadian players came up with the courage and strength to give it their best effort in the coming final game. But would you be surprised if I told you there was another problem before the final game?"

"No. There always seem to be problems all over the place! Now what happened?"

"As if there was not enough stress for Team Canada to deal with, the Soviets pulled another fast one before Game 8. Remember after the sixth game the Canadians were so upset about the officiating of the two West German referees, Baader and Kompalla, that they negotiated an agreement with the Soviets that the two referees in question would not officiate any more games?"

"Yeah..."

"At the press conference after Game 7, a reporter asked who the refs would be for the last game and Sinden said that it was all set and that an agreement was reached and the West German referees would not officiate any more games in the series. Soviet officials were there and heard him say that. None of them said anything or contradicted him. Well, the next day, on Wednesday, 27 September, the Soviets informed the Canadians that the West Germans were going to referee the last game. The Soviets unilaterally broke the agreement that they made with the Canadians after Game 6."

"How could they do that?"

"How? Well, the Canadian officials then met with one of the Soviet officials and reminded him that there was a commitment the Soviets were expected to live up to. However, the situation had changed and the Soviets no longer felt compelled to abide by the agreement. Before Game 7 the Soviets were sure they would win the series. Now that their victory was uncertain, they suddenly suggested that not having the German refs was discrimination and that they had never actually agreed to what the Canadians wanted. When the Canadians challenged that assertion, the Soviets said that something must have been missed or mixed up in the translation during their previous meeting. The Soviets were never short of excuses."

"So what did the Canadian officials do?"

"The Soviet and the Canadian officials did not resolve the matter that day but decided to follow up the next day before the game. During the following day's meeting on Thursday, September 28, the Canadians made it clear that they wanted the Swede Dahlberg and the Czechoslovak Bata to referee the final game as was previously agreed to. At one point during the meeting, Sinden told the Soviet officials that it was Dahlberg and Bata or no game. One of the Soviet officials looked at Sinden and said 'In Russia, we make the decisions, not you.'"

"So what happened? What did they do?"

"A Canadian embassy official who was acting as an interpreter suggested that each party select a referee as a compromise. The Soviets eventually agreed to that option and the Canadians realized that this was the best they could expect so they agreed and hoped the Soviets would not pull another switcheroo at game time. Do you think that was the end of the matter?"

"I hope so, but I guess not," Andy said as he shrugged his shoulders.

"The Soviets had another trick up their sleeve. When the Canadians picked Dahlberg, the Soviets immediately said that Dahlberg was unavailable because he was sick with the flu. The Canadians were suspicious. Eagleson who was at the meeting along with Sinden and Ferguson wrote in his book that he told the Soviets he had seen Dahlberg at breakfast that morning and Dahlberg was fine then. The Soviets claimed that Dahlberg became sick after he had had breakfast. Eagleson stepped out of the room and called Dahlberg to find out whether that was true. Dahlberg told Eagleson that a senior Soviet official who was the head of international referees for the International Ice Hockey Federation had told him that if he officiated the game he would never referee another international game. Accordingly, Dahlberg was informed that he was sick and would not be able to ref the game that evening."

"Holy smokes! Really?" Andy was surprised.

"Eagleson wrote that what Dahlberg told him had the ring of truth to it and that the Soviets were engaging in a ploy to ensure that their preferred referees would officiate the game. Between Dahlberg and Bata, the Soviets preferred Bata who was from a country under Soviet control at that time. Although the Soviets obviously had ways of exerting pressure on Dahlberg, they had even more ways of exerting pressure on anyone from a country under Soviet control which was the case with Czechoslovakia. The Canadian officials were eager to settle the matter so they picked Rudy Bata as their second choice."

"Who did the Soviets select?" Andy asked.

"The West German Josef Kompalla. The Canadians weren't surprised. Of all the European referees the Canadians considered Kompalla the worst. Sinden, Ferguson, and Eagleson had an incredible amount of patience and strength to deal with Soviet shenanigans throughout the series. If Dahlberg was really sick with the flu, where do you think he would be during the game that evening?"

"I guess he'd be in bed in his hotel room and watching the game on the television."

"When the game started, the Canadians saw Dahlberg sitting in the stands in plain sight."

CHAPTER 12:
GAME 8 IN MOSCOW

"So Andy, we've reached the end of the line and the biggest game of them all. Game 8 was on Thursday, September 28, 1972. It was a date that I will never forget. You can't imagine the tension and excitement that had built up across the country throughout the series and now reached a crescendo. From the moment I woke up that morning I felt as though I was experiencing an adrenaline rush and a feeling of intense excitement that lasted all day.

The broadcast started around noon. Every television in the country was turned on to the game and the whole country effectively shut down in the middle of a weekday so that an estimated 16 million Canadians out of a population of 22 million could watch the game. Televisions were set up in places where there were none before and people even gathered on sidewalks in front of electronics stores so they could watch the televisions on display in the store windows. Thousands of people called in sick at work so they could stay home and watch the game. I doubt very many managers and employers took the calls because they were probably calling in sick too.

In every school across Canada, televisions were set up in auditoriums, cafeterias, and classrooms so the kids would be able to watch the game. Although Mr. Cousineau had previously brought out a television so that we could watch Games 5 and 7, for this game our class would have to be satisfied with a radio. I can't remember if the problem was that there was a shortage of televisions in the school or whether Mr. Cousineau thought the reception on the television during the previous games was so bad that he did not want to endure that again, but he brought a small Sony transistor radio to class. In the morning we had our usual classes, but my classmates and I only had our minds on the game that was going to start soon. When the game started Mr. Cousineau placed the radio on his desk at the front of the class and turned it on so we could hear. Sometimes he would hold the radio up to his ear and tell us what he had just heard as the game went on. During the intermissions, we were supposed to work on our math workbook problems but I found concentrating on the math exercises to be impossible. I couldn't focus enough and wished I could just doodle in my art workbook instead. Most of my classmates felt the same way.

The referees for the final game were Rudy Bata and Josef Kompalla. As previously planned, Dryden was in nets. Sinden made another change to the lineup. Frank Mahovlich sat out the previous two games with a sore knee. He laced up for this game replacing Bill Goldsworthy. Kharlamov was in the Soviet lineup for the game. However, by all accounts, he was not in top form.

The first period started with penalties to Bill White at 2:25 and then Pete Mahovlich at 3:01. The Canadians felt that the two penalties were questionable and their worst fears about referee Kompalla seemed to be coming true. With a two-man advantage, Yakushev scored for the Soviets three and a half minutes into the game. The Soviets were up 0-1. Those first few minutes right at the start of the game had me and my classmates worried. You can imagine that the Canadian coaches and players wondered whether the start of this game was a sign of how the rest of the game would play out. Ten seconds later a Soviet got a hooking penalty. Then something really ugly happened."

"What?"

"A Soviet player had the puck at the Soviet blue line and was going by Jean-Paul Parisé. Parisé gave the Soviet player a shove and a second later the Soviet fell to the ice. Many viewers thought Parisé delivered a good check and that the Soviet player intentionally dived. The closest referee was Bata who waved his arms suggesting the play was fine. However, even though the Soviet player had the puck, Kompalla gave Parisé an interference penalty. That really upset the Canadians. How could Kompalla call interference on a player for trying to check the puck carrier? The Canadians were upset but none more than Parisé who swore at Kompalla and slammed his stick on the ice. Kompalla promptly awarded him a ten-minute misconduct penalty. Parisé then circled around on the ice and suddenly did something shocking."

"What did he do?"

"Kompalla was standing along the boards and Parisé charged toward him and raised his stick as if he were about to strike him with it. Fortunately, at the last second before reaching Kompalla, he lowered the stick and just kept mouthing off. For what he had done Parisé was ejected from the game. That was the right call. I wished he hadn't done that. However, the way the officiating was unfolding at the start of the game it seemed like Team Canada's worst fears about Kompalla being incompetent, biased against Team Canada, and doing everything he could to penalize them was coming true. Parisé's feelings of injustice and frustration were shared by the entire team. The game had just started and it didn't look like the officiating was going to be neutral and fair. The result was a huge outcry from the Canadian bench. Just as in Game 6 and in accordance with Sinden's philosophy about how to deal with awful officials, chairs were thrown onto the ice and the uproar lasted about ten minutes. Then the Canadians thought they had further proof that Kompalla didn't know what he was doing or was specifically targeting the Canadians."

"What did he do?"

"Parisé had been ejected from the game but another Canadian player had to sit out his penalty. Kompalla claimed that he could choose which player had to serve Parisé's penalty and... surprise, surprise... he picked Phil Esposito, Canada's leading scorer, to sit in the penalty box. Although Phil was on the ice when the infraction took place, the Canadian coaches had never heard of such a rule and refused to accept it. In the end, Dennis Hull served the two-minute minor for Parisé. Not only was Kompalla's neutrality in question so was his grasp of the rules. Guess how the Canadian fans in the stands reacted?"

"They started booing."

"Not quite. They started chanting 'Let's go home!' over and over. Tensions rose in the building as more Soviet soldiers and police showed up and the Canadian bench was surrounded by Soviet police. Can you believe that? Mr. Cousineau relayed the highlights of what he was hearing on the radio and we all tried to picture the scene. It sounded like chaos. It was a dreadful start to the game and there were still fifty-five minutes to go on the clock. Not surprisingly perhaps, the result of this fiasco was that Team Canada was even more determined to win."

"So what happened when they resumed playing?"

"Team Canada managed to kill off the penalty. Maybe all that uproar from the Canadian bench had an impact on the referees because at 6:28 Henderson was racing for the puck and this time a Soviet player got an interference penalty. During Canada's power play, Henderson got the puck in the Soviet corner and passed it to Lapointe at the blue line who passed it across to Park. Park one-timed it at the net. Tretiak stopped it but Phil Esposito got the rebound and put it away. Canada tied the game up at 1-1. When Mr. Cousineau told us that Canada had just scored we erupted in cheers!"

"All right Canada!" Andy exclaimed.

"Then there were more penalties. One for the Soviets at 9:46 and then one for Cournoyer at 12:51. While the Soviets were on a power play Vladimir Lutchenko scored making it 1-2. Every time we heard of a Soviet goal it was as though our teacher was giving us the worst possible news and we collectively booed. It was actually funny to listen to a classroom of kids saying 'booo'. I would have laughed had the circumstances not been so serious and the Soviets not taken the lead. Then, just before the seventeenth minute New York Ranger teammates Park and Ratelle passed the puck back and forth weaving their way through the Soviet defence. Park ended up firing the puck at an upper corner of the net to tie the game 2-2."

"Woo hoo! I bet your class cheered again!"

"Oh, big time! The first period action was back and forth all the way. We were relieved that Canada had come from behind to tie it up twice. There were forty minutes left in the game and Canada had yet to take the lead. Just as the first period started off badly for the Canadians, so did the second one. It wasn't because of the referees and the officiating though. In fact, the number of penalty calls during the rest of the game diminished. However, the Soviets charged towards the Canadian net and Yakushev fired the puck that went high over the net and bounced off the wire mesh. The rebound off the wire netting was like a slingshot and unlike anything off the Plexiglas in the NHL rinks. The Soviet players knew what it would do and how to use it. The puck flew by Dryden's head and landed in front of the net on Vladimir Shadrin's stick and he shot it in the net before Dryden could blink. All it took was twenty-one seconds and the Soviets were now leading 2-3."

"Aww..."

"When Mr. Cousineau told us the news I remember praying that the Canadians would not give up and would bounce back. I was sure they were doing their best. But boy was that fast goal at the start of the period unsettling. About ten minutes later Rod Gilbert took the puck along the boards towards a corner. He faked a shot and then passed it to White who was in the goal mouth. White tipped it over Tretiak for a goal. So halfway through the game, Canada had come from behind again to tie it up 3-3 and the class erupted in cheers. The game was approaching the halfway point and it was neck and neck but the tie did not last long. Just over a minute later the Soviets won a faceoff in the Canadian zone and the puck got to Yakushev who was alone in front of Dryden and he scored. The Soviets got the lead back at 11:43 and the score was 3-4."

"Not again!" Andy said in exasperation.

"It could have been worse! A few minutes later the Soviets put on more pressure in the Canadian zone and they managed to get the puck past Dryden. Just as it was about to cross the goal line Phil Esposito stopped it. Can you believe that? The team's centre came all the way back behind our goalie to prevent a goal. I remember when Mr. Cousineau told us that Phil Esposito prevented a Soviet goal I thought Phil Esposito was a genius. I was so glad he was on our team and not the Soviet one! Then Pat Stapleton got a cross-checking penalty just before the fifteenth-minute mark of the second period and Vasiliev scored a goal during the power play and the Soviets now had a 3-5 lead. That was the third Soviet power play goal of the game."

"I bet your class booed again."

"We sure did but this time it was more depressing than before. Team Canada was down by two goals. Then in the eighteenth minute, a Soviet player got an elbowing penalty. We prayed that the Canadians would score on the power play but they didn't."

"Aww. Too bad," Andy said.

"It was too bad all right. So the second period ended 3-5. The class was in an uptight mood, and I started to get annoyed with my teacher. When Mr. Cousineau gave us the news about the fourth and fifth Soviet goals, he was impassive and spoke as though it was expected. Although he tried to appear neutral in this contest, from the subtle nuances of his speech and tone I got the impression that he thought the Soviets were superior hockey players and ought to win. I hoped that Team Canada would emerge victorious and prove him wrong."

"Gramps, what would happen if the game ended in a tie? Would the series be declared to be a tie?"

"Another good question, Andy! During the second intermission, Alan Eagleson met one of the Soviet officials and commented that if the Canadians scored two goals and tied the game like the Soviets did back in Winnipeg, the game and the series would end in a tie and everyone would be happy. The Soviet official told Eagleson that if the game ended in a tie the Soviets would claim victory in the series because in international hockey when the games do not go into overtime the team that has the most goals in the tournament is declared the winner. That was the first time that such a possibility had been raised with the Canadians and they were unprepared for that scenario because that was not how ties were settled in the NHL. Again, they should have looked into tie-breaking rules and customs in international tournaments before and been aware that this was a possibility. When Eagleson heard that the Soviets would declare victory if the game ended in a tie, he went straight to the Canadian dressing room and gave the players a forceful pep talk encouraging them to score early in the next period. A tie game was not an option. Team Canada had to win the game to win the series."

"How did the players feel during the second intermission?"

"The players were not panicking or despairing. They were calm. They knew what they had to do and they knew they could do it. Each player knew that when their shift came up they would have to play the best hockey they had ever played in their lives."

"Sounds like overtime in the seventh game of the Stanley Cup finals."

"That's a good comparison. But this was bigger. There would always be another Stanley Cup final the next year. This was the first series of its kind and there would never be another 1972 Summit Series. It had been practically a full month since the fateful first game on September 2. In this final game, it all boiled down to the last period to determine who was going to win the series."

"Were you nervous, Gramps?"

"You better believe it! I was worried but also extremely excited. It seemed to me that absolutely nothing else mattered. Nothing! My classmates and I were focused only on what was going on in the game in Moscow. And we knew that we were not the only ones paying attention. The whole country was watching or listening to that game. What followed was, as far as I'm concerned, the most exciting and nerve-wracking twenty minutes of hockey ever played. So what did the Canadians have to do in the final period?"

"They had to prevent the Soviets from scoring any more goals and they had to score three to win," Andy replied.

"Exactly. Can you imagine the pressure on Dryden? If the Soviets scored another goal early in the period it would be unlikely the Canadians would be able to overcome such a deficit. The Canadian strategy was to continue to play a tight game and not open it up and take chances early because the Soviets might capitalize on a mistake. The key was to try to score a goal early in the period to narrow the Soviet lead. The third period started and the whole class listened in silence to the faint sound from Mr. Cousineau's radio at the front of the class and to his updates. So guess what happened?"

"Did Canada score a goal?"

"Yes! Just after the second minute of the third period Pete Mahovlich got the puck behind the Canadian net and passed it up to Cournoyer who passed it back to him. Mahovlich made his way up the boards to the corner beside the Soviet net. Mahovlich then got upended by a Soviet defender and as he fell he managed to pass the puck to Esposito at centre who managed to shoot it between Tretiak's pads. So at 2:27 of the third, the score was 4-5 and the Canadians managed to reduce the Soviet lead to just one goal. There were seventeen and a half minutes left."

"Go Canada go!" Andy blurted out.

"My classmates and I crossed our fingers that the Canadians would get another goal and tie the game soon. Then a few moments later at 3:41, a fight broke out between Rod Gilbert and a Soviet player. The Soviet player had raised Gilbert in the air and slammed him to the ice. Gilbert gave the Soviet player a bloody nose while he emerged unscathed. Both players got five minutes in the box but contrary to the usual international ban on fighting, neither was ejected from the game. The refs probably did not want to provoke another case of bedlam from the Canadian bench and just wanted to get through to the end of the game! Then at 4:27, the Soviets got a tripping penalty. This was a big chance for the Canadians to capitalize with the man advantage."

"Did they score?"

"Regrettably, they didn't. However, halfway through the period the Soviets started to adopt a more defensive shell approach hoping to protect their lead rather than trying to aggressively score again. The Soviets seemed to think that the worst thing that could happen was that Canada might score one more goal and tie the game, in which case the Soviets would claim to have won the series. Adopting that defensive shell turned out to be a gift to the Canadians. The clock was winding down and Mr. Cousineau's updates became more frequent and sometimes sounded like he was just repeating the play-by-play calls on the radio. I felt like a spring that was being compressed and the tension was driving me crazy! And then just before the thirteenth minute, the Canadians struck again!"

"What happened?" Andy asked excitedly.

"Esposito took a faceoff in the Canadian zone and got the puck to Park. Esposito took off in full stride. Park moved up and then shot a pass to Esposito who got it at centre and charged over the blue line. He fired a shot that Tretiak blocked but there was a rebound. Esposito knocked the puck out of the air and it went behind the net with Esposito in pursuit. He had three Soviets around him trying to get the puck but Esposito managed to shoot it toward Cournoyer in the centre. Tretiak blocked the pass and swept it back with his stick. Esposito tried again and fortunately, this time the puck got to Cournoyer who instantly shot at the net. Tretiak made the save but Cournoyer got the rebound and shot a backhander over Tretiak into the net. Canada tied the game 5-5!"

"Woo Hoo! Way to go Canada!" Andy blurted out as he got more and more animated.

"Oh, boy were we excited. When Mr. Cousineau told the class that Canada had scored and tied the game up we cheered louder than ever before. And we could hear the cheering from the other classrooms too! It was such a moment of euphoria. When he said that it was Cournoyer who scored the goal I was ecstatic with pride. My favourite player had come through when the team needed it most. But would you be surprised if I told you there was another complication?"

"No. What was it this time?"

"Remember in Game 7 when Henderson scored his amazing goal and the goal light did not come on?"

"Yeah. Ferguson and Sinden told all the players on the bench to get on the ice and celebrate with Henderson and the goal light came on, right?"

"Right! Well, even though the referee on the ice signaled that Cournoyer had just scored a goal, the goal light did not come on. The goal judge was a Soviet official. All the spectators in the arena saw the goal as well as the estimated more than 100 million television viewers. So why wouldn't the goal light come on?"

"Were the Soviets trying to say the goal did not count?"

"That's what worried some people. Alan Eagleson was in the stands and saw what was going on. Eagleson had previously noted that when the Soviets scored the goal light would stay on for about ten seconds. But when the Canadians scored the light would only come on for a second. So when the goal light did not come on at all this time he feared an attempt to deny Canada its goal. He immediately got up from his seat and tried to make his way to the official timer at ringside to ensure that the goal was announced and recorded but he didn't make it."

"What do you mean? Why didn't he make it?" Andy asked.

"The arena was full of uniformed soldiers, militia, police, and who knows how many plainclothes KGB security men. The soldiers around the rink should have known who Eagleson was but they didn't care. Two soldiers grabbed him and a couple of others started beating him. The soldiers then tried to hustle him out and take him somewhere. Can you imagine that happening to a Soviet official during the games in Canada? But the Soviets who held Eagleson encountered something they did not expect."

"What was that?"

"Pete Mahovlich was on the ice and was tall enough to see above the crowd and see Eagleson being held and taken away. Mahovlich yelled at his teammates for help while he jumped over the boards in an attempt to rescue Eagleson. Sinden wrote that

Mahovlich threatened the Soviets holding Eagleson with his stick. Eagleson later wrote that Mahovlich went further than that and hit one soldier with his stick and speared another one. If that's true, Mahovlich sure had a lot of guts! Other Canadian players skated over in alarm and bunched up along the boards where Mahovlich was trying to free Eagleson. Fortunately, the Soviets released Eagleson and Mahovlich escorted him onto the ice and toward the Canadian bench where they hoped he would be safe from the overly eager Soviet security personnel. As Eagleson crossed the ice with his rescuers the Soviet crowd in the stands started whistling, which was their way of booing, while the Canadian fans were cheering. Eagleson shook his fist at the goal judge and at least one member of the team staff then displayed a rude gesture using his finger to the Soviet crowd."

"That was not very nice."

"True. Although the rude gesture was embarrassing, the way Eagleson was treated was crazy. Soviet hockey officials should have been more helpful and the whole thing could have been completely avoided if the goal judge had simply turned on the light and the announcer announced the goal without any unnecessary delay. Anyway, that incident further riled the Canadian bench just like the Parisé episode did in the first period. Ferguson wrote that it had a positive psychological effect on the team and that they were now more determined than ever to win the game!

There were seven minutes and four seconds left on the clock and now that the game was tied the Soviets decided to come out of their defensive shell and both teams played flat out and exerted pressure back and forth. I was so fearful of the Soviets scoring that if I had been my current age at that time, I would probably have had a heart attack! Dennis Hull and Vladimir Petrov both got penalties at 15:24. The clock kept winding down. These last few minutes of the game were turning into a real nail-biter. The whole class was looking at Mr. Cousineau who held his little Sony transistor radio close to his ear and relayed the updates to us. We all quietly listened and crossed our fingers. During those last minutes, I prayed that the Canadians would score again. They only needed one more. But I knew that anything could happen. The Soviets could score and spoil everything. Both the Canadians and the Soviets wanted to score the winning goal, but there was a difference."

"What was that?" Andy asked.

"Remember what I said about playing with heart and soul? The Canadians played with more urgency. They wanted the victory more. Serge Savard would later say in an interview that the Soviets did not play with the emotion that the Canadians had and he could see it in their eyes. It was as though the Soviet players knew they were going to lose. And then it happened."

"Then what happened?" Andy asked excitedly.

"The clock was winding down and there was just a minute left in the game. The Esposito-Cournoyer-Pete Mahovlich line was nearing the end of its shift. Instead of waiting for Sinden to send him on the ice, Henderson called out to Mahovlich to come off. Henderson had never done anything like that before but he had a feeling that he could score in the last minute. Mahovlich responded to Henderson's call and came off the ice while Henderson jumped over the boards to join the action with just seconds left in the game. At that point, the puck was behind the Soviet net and a Soviet player tried to clear it out of the zone along the boards. Cournoyer was at the blue line and stopped the puck. Henderson screamed at him for a pass. Henderson had a clear shot at the net and would have one-timed it but Cournoyer's cross-ice pass went just behind Henderson. Henderson tried to reach back for the puck but his momentum was carrying him forward. He missed the puck and a Soviet defenceman tripped him causing him to fall and slide into the boards behind the net. The puck bounced off the boards in the corner. The three Soviet players there had a great opportunity to clear the puck out of the zone but none of them managed to take possession. Esposito whacked the loose puck toward the Soviet net. Tretiak blocked the shot with his stick but couldn't smother it. In the meantime, Henderson got up and was right there in the crease to pick up the rebound. Henderson tried to slide a shot along the ice, but Tretiak made a pad save and the puck went right back to Henderson. There were just 34 seconds left in the game. Tretiak was now stretched out on his back and Henderson shot the puck into the net."

"He scored!"

"He most certainly did! That was the most famous goal in Canadian hockey history! In the famous words spoken by the legendary Foster Hewitt: 'Cournoyer has it on that wing. Here's a shot – Henderson made a wild stab for it and fell. Here's another shot! Right in front – THEY SCORE!!! Henderson has scored for Canada!' I've got goosebumps now just thinking about how beautiful that moment was.

Right then Henderson turned around toward the Canadian bench and jumped up with his hands and stick in the air and Cournoyer was the first to wrap his arms around him in a bear hug. There were a couple of Canadian photojournalists at rink side who were capturing the drama throughout the series with their cameras. One of them was Frank Lennon and right at that moment he took one of the most famous photographs in Canadian history."

"That's the one on the wall in your study!"

"That's the one! And at that moment I think the entire country jumped out of their seats in celebration and I was sure that we all caused an earthquake that could be felt in China. Every Canadian hockey fan who was watching the game had their hands in the air and was cheering. My class and all the other classes in the school erupted in celebration with cheers when Henderson scored that goal. I remember feeling not only a sense of tremendous relief but that something larger than life had happened. Once we all came back to earth, we realized that the game was still not over! The score was 6-5 but there were still thirty-four seconds left on the clock and anything could happen! It was the most nerve-wracking thirty-four seconds of my life! Fortunately, the Soviets did not score, and when the final buzzer sounded the country again erupted in jubilation! The game and the series were over. Canada came out on top! We won! Let me tell you, on September 28, 1972, it felt great to be a Canadian! All the tension and worry and fear that I had felt since that first game on September 2 had vanished in a split second.

We were so excited in class after the victory and I must have cheered the loudest because once the celebrating settled down Mr. Cousineau got up from his chair at the front of the class and took a few steps towards me and said 'You know, Floyd, the Soviets played better than the Canadians.' I responded by saying that usually the better team wins and Canada did just that. Team Canada made me so proud to be a Canadian!

While Canadians across the country were celebrating the victory, Team Canada had their own celebration in Moscow. After all they had been through, they had earned it! The Soviets had previously arranged for a 'victory' party at the Metropole Hotel in Moscow for all the players from both teams after the final game. All the Canadians showed up but only two Soviet players did, Yakushev and Tretiak. Yakushev received an award as the best forward in the series. Park was similarly recognized as the best defenceman. The Canadians went back to their hotel and let loose. And they were happy to leave Moscow the next day. Sinden said afterward 'The best day in your life is the day you leave this place.' The team was exhausted, but they still had one more exhibition game on their schedule to play in Prague on September 30 before returning to Canada."

"How did that game go?" Andy queried.

"For the Canadians, the game in Prague was somewhat of an anticlimax after what they had just been through. However, they did not want to lose. The Czechoslovak national team was not as good as the Soviet one but they had beaten the Soviets and won the World Championship earlier that year. Toward the end of the game, Team Canada was losing 3-4. Fortunately, in the final seconds, Phil Esposito scored to tie the game up 4-4. The team was glad to have pulled off the tie."

"Well, that's better than a loss. Good for them!"

"After the exhibition game in Prague, the team flew home. The flight first landed at Dorval and was greeted by the Prime Minister and a huge crowd of fans. Henderson wrote that the crowd was massive and the airport was a madhouse which went even crazier when the team got off the plane and got on some fire trucks that circled around the tarmac. The Montreal players stayed in Montreal while the rest of the team flew on to Toronto. When the plane arrived in Toronto Phil Esposito showed just how happy he was to be back home. He walked down the stairs from the plane and kissed the tarmac! The team was then driven to Nathan Phillips Square downtown where 80,000 people greeted them in the rain! I wish I could have been there to join the crowd when they sang 'O Canada'.

I was so proud of Team Canada. The whole country was proud of them. They did more for national unity and making everyone feel like we were in this together. It was one of those moments when, in my youthful mind, there was justice in the natural order of things and the good guys won. After that series was over, I was in a cloud of joy that lasted for weeks.

Sinden wrote 'The greatest hockey I have ever witnessed was played during our Team Canada-Russia series. It was unmatched in the annals of the game for continuous action. The Russians pushed us to the limit, but at the same time we induced the Soviets to bring their game to a peak.'

In his memoirs, Phil Esposito wrote: 'Looking back, it was one hell of a series. It was the toughest thing I ever had to do in my life as a hockey player. The mental anguish we all went through was overwhelming. And I never was able to play at that level again.'

For many Canadian hockey fans who followed the Summit Series, the performance of the members of Team Canada was without any doubt, to use one of Winston Churchill's famous lines, 'Their finest hour'. That Summit Series was one of the most special memories from my youth. The guys on Team Canada were the best. Ever." Floyd thought for a moment and then added, "Period."

"Thanks, Gramps. That was an awesome story."

"You're welcome, Andy, but hold on! It isn't over!"

CHAPTER 13:
CANADA'S
TEAM OF THE CENTURY

"So what was the final tally in the Summit Series?" Floyd asked.

"Canada won four games, the Soviets three, and there was one tie," Andy replied.

"That's right. the Soviets scored 32 goals in total and the Canadians 31. To many observers, the two teams proved to be each other's equal. Both teams learned a lot by observing how the other team played the game. The Soviets were models of conditioning perfection and were superior in most facets of the game, especially passing and set team plays. Canadian hockey players who wanted to be the best they could be inevitably had to adopt some chapters from the Soviet training book."

"What did the Soviets learn from the Canadians?"

"Sinden wrote that the only hockey skill where the Canadians were superior to the Soviets was shooting. However, he also added that the Canadians were tougher mentally and their mental conditioning helped them win the series."

"Mental conditioning? What did he mean, Gramps?"

"He thought that the reason the Canadians won was because they knew how to play the big game. Canadians were more accustomed to playing games where there was more at stake than the Soviets were. The Canadians had the kind of mental toughness that only comes from playing in something like the NHL playoffs and the Stanley Cup finals. That was a determining factor that helped Team Canada win the last three games.

However, even though the game scores suggest the teams were more or less equal, when you consider the details and context of what happened during the Summit Series, some people have suggested that that teams were not really that equal and that the Soviets were overrated while the Canadians were underrated."

"What do they base that on, Gramps?"

"Well, the initial April agreement with the Soviets gave them several advantages and the team encountered all kinds of unexpected challenges that we already discussed. However, one of the biggest challenges the Canadian players faced in the series was the penalties. Even though the Canadians played their usual NHL style of hockey, they were more frequently penalized than the Soviets were. In his fiftieth anniversary book about the series titled *The Series*, Ken Dryden wrote 'All the penalties we were getting, we deserved more than they did, but *that many* more?' and Dryden used italics in the words 'that many' for emphasis."

"How many more penalties did the Canadians get than the Soviets?"

"I did not realize this until I came across some books with pages of statistics about the series and found out that if you add up the total number of penalty minutes, the Soviets got 84 minutes while the Canadians got 147 minutes. The difference is 63 minutes."

"Holy smokes! That's more than a whole game!"

"Exactly! Being short-handed for so much more time than the Soviets were was a huge handicap for the Canadians! If the two teams were equal, with such a huge advantage, the Soviets should have beaten the Canadians. But they didn't. Despite being in the penalty box so much more than the Soviets, the Canadians still won the series. I wish I had known these penalty statistics at the end of the series so that I could have pointed them out to Mr. Cousineau when he said that the Soviet team played better. Imagine if the tables had been turned and the Soviets had been the ones with the bigger number of penalties."

"The Canadians would have probably scored a few more goals," Andy surmised.

"I suspect so too. Under the circumstances, it seems that the Canadian players deserve even more credit and recognition for what they accomplished. Team Canada staged the greatest comeback in Canadian sports history, and in the process taught all the kids of my generation an important life lesson on how to deal with adversity."

"How?"

"With grit, determination, courage, and self-confidence. The team spirit that Team Canada exemplified was fantastic. After the series, I got a copy of the photograph of Paul Henderson celebrating his winning goal and have always had a copy on the wall at home. To me, that picture symbolizes the spirit of never giving up and fighting to the last second. Throughout my life that photograph has provided me with an endless source of inspiration. I love that photograph."

"Wow, Gramps. I want to get a copy of that picture to put on the wall in my room too!"

"We'll get you one. Now that you know the story behind it, I'm sure you will appreciate it more. Now, there's a few final things I want to tell you about Team Canada's legacy. Every year the sports writers of the Canadian Press conduct a poll to determine the nation's top team which is then recognized with the Canadian Press 'Team of the Year Award'. Guess which team won the award in 1972?

"I think it's kinda obvious, Gramps."

"It certainly was in 1972. And in 1999 the Canadian Press conducted another poll and designated Team Canada 1972 the 'Team of the Century'. There is a beautiful monument honouring the team right in front of the Hockey Hall of Fame in Toronto."

"I want to see it!"

"You probably already have but didn't realize the significance at the time. Just tell your parents you want to visit the Hockey Hall of Fame again and get them to take you on a trip to Toronto! And guess what the Canadian Press also designated as the 'Sports Moment of the Century'?"

"Was it Henderson's goal in Game 8?"

"It sure was. Frank Lennon's photograph of Henderson celebrating that goal also won a National Newspaper Award and was named Canadian Press 'Photograph of the Year'."

Floyd took a deep breath and sighed. "It's hard to believe it all happened fifty years ago. I remember it as though it was yesterday." He then added, "Well, Andy, that was the story of the 1972 hockey showdown."

"That was a great story, Gramps. Thanks for telling it to me."

"You're welcome, Andy. Down the road, I hope you'll enjoy telling the story to your children and grandchildren as much as I enjoyed telling it to you!"

THE PHOTOGRAPH

Credit: Frank Lennon / Library and Archives Canada / e008440339. Copyright: Estate of Frank Lennon. Reproduced with permission.

FURTHER READING

Bacon, John U. *The Greatest Comeback: How Team Canada Fought Back, Took the Summit Series, and Reinvented Hockey.* (New York: HarperCollins, 2022).

Bendell, Richard J. with Paul Patskou & Robert MacAskill. *1972 The Summit Series: Canada vs. USSR, Stats, Lies & Videotape, The Untold Story of Hockey's Series of the Century.* (n.p.: n.p., 2012).

Bidini, Dave. *A Wild Stab for It: This Is Game Eight from Russia.* (Toronto: ECW Press, 2012).

Brignall, Richard. *Summit Series '72: Eight Games That Put Canada on Top of World Hockey.* (Toronto: James Lorimer & Company Ltd., 2011).

Dryden, Ken. *Face-Off at the Summit.* (Toronto: Little, Brown & Company, 1973).

Dryden, Ken. *The Series.* (Toronto: McClelland & Stewart, 2022).

Eagleson, Alan with Scott Young. *Power Play: The Memoirs of Hockey Czar Alan Eagleson.* (Toronto: McClelland & Stewart, 1991).

Ellis, Ron & Kevin Shea. *Over the Boards: The Ron Ellis Story.* (Bolton, ON: Fenn Publishing Co. Ltd., 2002).

Esposito, Phil & Peter Golenbock. *Thunder and Lightning: A No-B.S. Hockey Memoir.* (Toronto: McClelland & Stewart, 2003).

Franke, Greg. *Epic Confrontation: Canada vs. Russia on Ice: The Greatest Sports Drama of All Time.* (New York: Page Publishing, Inc., 2018).

Ferguson, John with Stan & Shirley Fischler. *Thunder and Lightning.* (Scarborough, Ontario: Prentice-Hall Canada, Inc., 1989).

Gault, John. *The Fans Go Wild: Paul Henderson's Miracle.* (Toronto: The Alger Press Ltd., 1973).

Hadfield, Vic & Tim Moriarty. *Vic Hadfield's Diary: From Moscow to the Play-offs.* (Garden City, N.Y.: Doubleday & Company, Inc., 1974).

Henderson, Paul with Mike Leonetti. *Shooting for Glory.* (Toronto: Stoddart Publishing Co. Limited., 1992).

Henderson, Paul with Roger Lajoie. *The Goal of My Life: A Memoir.* (Toronto: McClelland & Stewart, 2012).

Hoppener, Henk W. *Death of a Legend: Summer of '72 Team Canada vs. USSR Nationals.* (Montreal: Copp Clark Publishing Company, 1972).

Hughes, Aaron W. *10 Days That Shaped Modern Canada.* (Edmonton, Alberta: University of Alberta Press, 2022).

Hull, Dennis. *The Third Best Hull: I Should Have Been Fourth But They Wouldn't Let My Sister Maxine Play.* (Toronto: ECW Press, 1998).

Kennedy, Brian (ed.). *Coming Down the Mountain: Rethinking the 1972 Summit Series.* (Hamilton: Wolsak & Wynn, 2014).

Leonetti, Mike. *The Greatest Goal.* (Toronto: Scholastic Canada Ltd., 2001).

Leonetti, Mike. *Titans of '72: Team Canada's Summit Series Heroes.* (Toronto: Dundurn, 2012).

Ludwig, Jack. *Hockey Night in Moscow.* (Toronto: McClelland and Stewart Limited, 1972).

Ludwig, Jack. *The Great Hockey Thaw or The Russians Are Here!* (Garden City, New York: Doubleday & Company, Inc., 1974).

MacFarlane, John. *Team Canada 1972: Where Are They Now?* (Etobicoke: Winding Stair Press, 2001).

MacFarlane, John. *Twenty-seven Days in September: The Official Hockey Canada History of the 1972 Canada/U.S.S.R. Series.* (n.p.: Hockey Canada and Prosport Productions Limited, 1973).

MacSkimming, Roy. *Cold War: The Amazing Canada-Soviet Hockey Series of 1972.* (Vancouver: Douglas & McIntyre, 1996).

Mahovlich, Ted. *The Big M: The Frank Mahovlich Story.* (Toronto: HarperCollins Canada, 1999).

Martin, Lawrence. *The Red Machine: The Soviet Quest to Dominate Canada's Game.* (Toronto: Doubleday Canada Limited, 1990).

McKee, Taylor (ed.). *Reaching the Summit: Reimagining the Summit Series in the Canadian Cultural Memory.* (n.p.: JESS Press, 2022).

Mitton, Sean & Jim Prime. *The Goal That United Canada: 72 Amazing Stories by Canadians From Coast to Coast.* (n.p.: n.p., 2022).

Mitton, Sean, Paul Patskou & Alex Braverman. *When Canada Shut Down: 72 Amazing Untold Stories From A Canadian And Soviet Perspective.* (n.p.: n.p., 2022).

Morrison, Scott. *1972: The Series That Changed Hockey Forever.* (Toronto: Simon & Shuster Canada, 2022).

Morrison, Scott. *The Days Canada Stood Still: Canada vs USSR 1972.* (Toronto: McGraw-Hill Ryerson Limited, 1989).

Podnieks, Andrew. *Team Canada 1972: The Official 40th Anniversary Celebration of the Summit Series, As Told by the Players.* (Toronto: McClelland & Stewart, 2012).

Prime, Jim. *Ice Dreams: The 1972 Summit Series, 50 Years On.* (Annapolis County, NS: Moose House Publications, 2022).

Savard, Serge. *Serge Savard: Forever Canadien.* (Montreal: KO Éditions inc., 2020).

Sears, Thom & Brad Park. *Straight Shooter: The Brad Park Story.* (Mississauga, ON: John Wiley & Sons Canada, Ltd., 2012).

Sinden, Harry. *Hockey Showdown: The Canada-Russia Hockey Series.* (Toronto: Doubleday Canada Ltd., 1972).

Smith, Gary J. *Ice War Diplomat: Hockey Meets Cold War Politics at the 1972 Summit Series.* (Madeira Park, B.C.: Douglas & McIntyre (2013) Ltd., 2022).

Terroux, Gilles. *Le match du siècle: Canada-U.R.S.S.* (Montréal: Les Éditions de L'Homme, 1972.) Published in English as *Face-Off of the Century: Canada-U.S.S.R., A New Era.* (Toronto?: Collier-Macmillan Canada, 1972.)

Request to Readers:
If you enjoyed this book, please take a few moments to write a review on the book's Amazon page.

https://www.amazon.ca/1972-Hockey-Showdown-story-Gramps-ebook/dp/B0CFG72S2V/ref=tmm_kin_swatch_0?_encoding=UTF8 &qid=1692445707&sr=8-1

Thank you!

Made in the USA
Columbia, SC
29 October 2023

25149838R00085